Instructor's Manual with Test Bank to Accompany
INTRODUCTION TO PRIVATE SECURITY

Fourth Edition

Kären M. Hess
Normandale Community College
Bloomington, Minnesota

Henry M. Wrobleski
Private Security Investigator
and Evaluator
Edina, Minnesota

Prepared by
Christine M. H. Orthmann
Innovative Programming Systems, Inc.
North Lauderdale, Florida

West Publishing Company

St. Paul   New York   Los Angeles   San Francisco

WEST'S COMMITMENT TO THE ENVIRONMENT

In 1906, West Publishing Company began recycling materials left over from the production of books. This began a tradition of efficient and responsible use of resources. Today, 100% of our legal bound volumes are printed on acid-free, recycled paper consisting of 50% new paper pulp and 50% paper that has undergone a de-inking process. We also use vegetable-based inks to print all of our books. West recycles nearly 27,700,000 pounds of scrap paper annually—the equivalent of 229,300 trees. Since the 1960s, West has devised ways to capture and recycle waste inks, solvents, oils, and vapors created in the printing process. We also recycle plastics of all kinds, wood, glass, corrugated cardboard, and batteries, and have eliminated the use of polystyrene book packaging. We at West are proud of the longevity and the scope of our commitment to the environment.

West pocket parts and advance sheets are printed on recyclable paper and can be collected and recycled with newspapers. Staples do not have to be removed. Bound volumes can be recycled after removing the cover.

Production, Prepress, Printing and Binding by West Publishing Company.

TEXT IS PRINTED ON 10% POST CONSUMER RECYCLED PAPER   Printed with Printwise
Environmentally Advanced Water Washable Ink

COPYRIGHT © 1996 by   WEST PUBLISHING CO.
610 Opperman Drive
P.O. Box 64526
St. Paul, MN 55164–0526

All rights reserved
Printed in the United States of America
03 02 01 00 99 98 97 96   8 7 6 5 4 3 2 1 0

ISBN 0–314–06977–1

CONTENTS

		Page
Introduction		v
1	The Evolution of Private Security: A Brief History	1
2	Modern Private Security: An Overview	5
3	The Public/Private Interface and Legal Authority	9
4	Legal Liability	13
5	Enhancing Security Through Physical Controls	17
6	Enhancing Security Through Procedural Controls	21
7	Preventing Losses from Accidents and Emergencies	25
8	Preventing Losses from Criminal Actions	29
9	Enhancing Information/Computer Security	33
10	Enhancing Public Relations	37
11	The Investigative Function	41
12	Obtaining and Providing Information	45
13	Testifying in Court	49
14	Loss Prevention Through Risk Management	53
15	Industrial Security	57
16	Retail Security	61
17	Commercial Security	65
18	Institutional Security	69
19	Other Applications of Security at Work	73
20	The Challenges of Violence in the Workplace	77
21	Practicing and Promoting Ethical Conduct	81
22	The Private Security Professional and Profession	85
23	A Look to the Future	89
Chapter Quizzes		93

INTRODUCTION

This manual is designed as an aid in using *Introduction To Private Security*. For each chapter of the text you are provided:

- Chapter objectives
- Key terms
- Possible responses to the application exercises
- Possible answers to the discussion questions
- An objective chapter quiz and answers
- Space for notes

The applications are designed to give students an opportunity to apply the basic concepts of the chapter in a hypothetical situation. The answers provided are only a start. In most instances they can be expanded on at much greater length.

The brief answers given for the discussion questions are, again, only a start, designed as a springboard for further discussion. Often there will be as many answers to a question as there are students in your class.

The quizzes are designed to give you and your students feedback on their progress in mastering the chapter's objectives. They are placed at the end of this manual to facilitate duplicating copies for classroom use. Feel free to reproduce the quizzes as they are printed or to modify them as you see fit. If you want more extensive feedback, you might use the chapter objectives in total or selected objectives as the basis for a quiz in which the students write brief responses to each "Do you know..." question.

For some chapters, suggested audio-visual aids to use in conjunction with the text are provided. Also for several chapters, additional information to supplement the textual information is included.

Each chapter can be expanded based on your extensive knowledge of the subjects covered and your personal experience. Following are some specific suggestions you might want to implement with some or all of the chapters.

1. Have students write on 3" x 5" notecards any questions they have while reading the chapter, to be turned in to you for class discussion. In this way you can reach each student personally and develop an awareness of interest areas for the entire class.

2. Have students review newspapers and magazines and clip examples of the key concepts in the chapter, especially new cases that might change present laws. The same might be done for currently popular television shows dealing with private security and how these shows represent or distort reality. Since no text can be completely current, it must be supplemented by recent incidents and court decisions provided by you and your students.

3. Have students relate personal experiences they have had with the concepts or procedures described in a specific chapter.

4. Present illustrative examples from your experience that demonstrate the principles presented in the chapter.

5. Assign research subjects to groups of three to five students. Appoint a leader to report the group's findings to the entire class. Some controversial topics might serve as the basis for classroom debates.

6. Invite outside representatives of diverse opinions on a given subject to speak to the class. For example, you might invite the director of a contractual security force and the director of a proprietary security force to discuss with your class the advantages of their particular kind of security.

7. Invite security officers/managers from your area to present current information and some actual cases. They might discuss a specific security problem, the risks involved, and how these risks have been minimized.

8. Obtain audio-visual materials on the topics from local public and law enforcement libraries.

9. Check security magazines for articles on specific subjects. Such articles can provide varied viewpoints of experts in the field.

10. Select additional readings for students wishing to pursue a subject in greater depth. Many suggestions are contained in the reference section at the end of each chapter. You might arrange for extra-credit reports, either oral or written, to be shared with the class.

Following are additional tools concerning the preparation of written assignments, the completion of case reviews and the fulfillment of final project requirements. A sample grading sheet is also provided. These tools may be use with your class and modified to suit your needs (Courtesy of Professor Diane Zahm, Florida State University).

⇒ **Preparing Written Assignments for Class**

When preparing written assignments for class, assume that you have been hired as a consultant and your audience is your professional client. This person will be concerned primarily with ACTION, not INFORMATION. Thus, the report should only include enough background information to understand the findings and recommended actions.

Also, consider this: a consultant's reputation rests on the quality of the work s/he submits. Reports with misspelled words, bad grammar or inaccurate or incomplete information, no matter how good the recommendations, will leave the consultant with a bad reputation--and unpaid and unemployed. Attention to detail is critical (and counts for 40% of the grade on the final project, for example).

1. Written work *must* follow the guidelines in the *Publication Manual of the American Psychological Association*. Please refer to this manual for style and format.

2. All assignments must be typed, double-spaced.

3. Student name and assignment date should appear in the top left corner of all pages and a page number should be provided in the top right corner of each page.

4. Only pica (12 point) or elite (10 point) type are acceptable.

5. Students must attach the following (including their signatures) to all work turned in during the semester:

> *On my honor, I pledge that I have neither given nor received any assistance on this assignment exam.*

Students who do not sign a pledge are admitting the work is not original, and a failing grade will be assigned to the work.

Any work not meeting the style requirements outlined in this syllabus, including the length or other requirements for the assignment, will receive a reduced grade.

⇒ Case Review Sheet

Name the type of land use/facility under consideration:

Who uses this place?

What assets must be protected at this location?

      a.

      b.

      c.

      d.

      e.

What types of crimes are most likely to occur at this location? (Consider all crimes, not just the crimes identified in the case.)

a.

b.

c.

d.

Is there anything about this place that makes it unique with regard to liability? What is this?

What is the "problem" in this case?

Who are the victims?

What costs are involved as the result of the crime or other problem?

Is there something about the physical environment/design that causes this problem to occur? What is it?

Are there rules or policies that contribute to the problem? What are these?

What alternatives are available to address or correct the problem?

    a. What changes to the design and layout?

    b. What physical or electronic security measures?

    c. What changes to policies and procedures?

Which alternative was selected?

Why was it chosen?

What happened because the alternative was implemented?

⇒ **Final Project Requirements**

Step #1: Select a location for your semester project. The location should be of a "manageable" size; therefore, do not select an entire mall. You may select a single store in the mall, although this, too, is discouraged.

The location name, its address, a contact person and a contact phone number must be turned in to the instructor on (date).

Step #2: Neighborhood/Area review. The purpose of this step is to help you get a "feel" for the area surrounding your location.

a. Take a walk or ride in the neighborhood surrounding your site (I would do both). Things to look at:

- existing land use
- traffic, public transportation and parking
- resident and business demographics
- clues as to neighborhood character and stability.

While you are doing this, try to get the big picture of the neighborhood. DO NOT be concerned with crime or safety.

b. Prepare one or more maps to document your findings, e.g., land use map, transportation map, problem areas map, demographics map.

Step #3: Behavioral Project. For this step, go to the location you selected.

a. Walk around the facility and look at the physical site layout. Draw a plan of the site, showing the location of the building, parking (if any), driving lanes, lighting, signs, etc.

b. Walk around the inside of the facility and look at its design. Draw a floor plan of the location and identify details on the plan, e.g., layout, mode of display, colors, lighting, relative location of items, etc.

c. Set up a system for observing and recording behavior. Once your system is in place observe behavior and record this for at least **1 HOUR**. Use a copy of your floor plan to document your findings. Please record the start and end time for your observation.

Step #4: Crime/Risk Analysis.

a. Gather crime data for the location and the surrounding area from the local police department, the library or UCR. Develop a matrix, table, graph or chart using this information.

b. Talk to the manager and employees (if any). Ask about their experiences, roles and responsibilities, current policies and procedures, etc. Write 5-10 "bullet" statements summarizing this information.

c. Conduct a user survey on fear and victiminzation. Create a table, graph or chart summarizing your findings.

d. Use the tables, graphs, charts and other information to look for crime patterns or trends.

e. Identify any crime risks the owner should consider as part of a crime prevention/security program for the location.

Step #5: Crime Prevention/Security Evaluation. Gather information on the crime prevention/security program now in place at the location. This information should include:

- person in charge of or responsible for crime and loss prevention or security
- physical and electronic security survey
- inventory of crime and loss prevention or security policies and procedures
- how long the policy or program has been in existence
- whether any security measures have been evaluated
- the results of the evaluation.

FINAL PROJECT: At long last, it is time to draw some conclusions and make some recommendations regarding the location. The project should be no more than 6 pages long, plus graphics or other supporting material. It consists of three major parts, based on your earlier work:

Part I--Introduction and Background

- identifies and describes the location
- describes the surrounding environment
- outlines the method used, including sources of data, times visited, etc.
- presents crime data
- presents design and behavior information
- describes the crime prevention and security measures now in place, including policies and procedures

Part II--Crime/Environment Relationships (findings, problems or issues, both positive and negative)

- identifies any legal issues that are unique to this particular establishment
- discusses the strengths and weaknesses discovered in crime prevention programs, policies or procedures
- describes any potential crime problems or crime risks at the site

Part III--Conclusions and Recommendations

- tells the reader what needs to be done to reduce the risk of crime and loss, including
  - program modifications
  - changes to policy
  - new or different physical or electronic security measures
  - design modifications
- also describes how any changes should be evaluated to determine their effectiveness, when this evaluation should take place

SOME HINTS:

1. Use graphics to your best advantage. Put the most important information in the text, e.g., crime data. For less important information, refer readers to the maps, tables and charts, and let them gather as much information as possible on their own from the graphics. (Remember, if you attach something to the paper, you *must* refer to it somewhere in the paper.)

2. The Conclusions and Recommendations section is the focus of the report and should take up the greatest amount of space. Concentrate on using numbered recommendations or bullet statements. Focus on ACTIONS that should be taken. Be as specific as you possibly can.

3. If you make a recommendation, you *must* have (a) data in Part I and (b) a finding in Part II to justify the recommendation. Alternatively, if you have a finding in Part II, you *must* have a recommendation action in Part III.

⇒ Grading Sheet

NAME: _____

CENTRAL THEME/ARGUMENT
    The paper presents a clearly defined argument (5 points)
    The paper infers an argument but does not clarify it (3 points)
    There is no central theme. or argument. in the paper (0 points)
    ARGUMENT POINTS .... _____

DOCUMENTATION/SUPPORT
    The argument is supported by documented or well-known facts (5 points)
    The argument appears factual but does not incorporate specific documentation (3 points)
    The argument relies entirely on the opinions of the author (0 points)
    DOCUMENTATION POINTS .... _____

CLARITY OF THOUGHT
    The paper is well-organized and there is a logical and constant flow of information (5 points)
    There are inconsistencies in the information presented (3 points)
    The paper lacks any organization and the information it presents is difficult to follow (0 points)
    CLARITY POINTS .... _____

GRAMMAR, SPELLING AND PUNCTUATION
    The paper is free of errors (5 points)
    The paper generally uses correct grammar and punctuation (3 points)
    The paper contains numerous spelling and other errors which have not been corrected (0 points)
    GRAMMAR POINTS .... _____

STYLE
    The paper follows the style and length guidelines provided by the instructor (5 points)
    The paper meets length requirements but does not use the appropriate style (3 points)
    The paper uses the style guidelines defined for the assignment but fails to meet its
        length requirement (2 points)
    The paper does not meet the required guidelines (0 points)
    STYLE POINTS .... _____

TOTAL POINTS (25 maximum) .... _____

If you have comments or suggestions for improving this manual or the text, we would like to hear from you.

Kären M. Hess
Henry M. Wrobleski

Normandale Community College
9700 France Avenue South
Bloomington, MN 55431

Chapter 1

THE EVOLUTION OF PRIVATE SECURITY: A BRIEF HISTORY

OBJECTIVES

Upon completing this chapter, the student will know:

- Generally how private security has differed from public law enforcement throughout history.

- What security measures were used in ancient times, in the Middle Ages, in eighteenth-century England and in early colonial America.

- What security measure were established by the tithing system, the Frankpledge system, the Magna Charta and the Statute of Westminster.

- What contributions to private security were made by Henry Fielding, Patrick Colquhoun, Sir Robert Peel, Allan Pinkerton, Washington Perry Brink, William J. Burns and George Wackenhut.

- What role the railroad police played in the evolution of private security.

- What impact the world wars had on the evolution of private security.

- Into what status private security has evolved by the 1990s.

KEY TERMS

The student will also be able to define the following terms: assize of arms, Bow Street Runners, feudalism, Frankpledge system, hue and cry, Magna Charta, parish, private security, Statute of Westminster, tithings, watch and ward.

POSSIBLE RESPONSES TO THE APPLICATION

1. Answers will vary considerably to what facts students will include in a talk to a college class on "The Evolution of Private Security" and what they will choose to stress. Students can check their answers by comparing them with the boxed information or the summary at the end of the chapter.

2. As with the first application, students will vary considerably in the facts they would include in a talk to a class at the local police academy on the historical role of private security as it related to early public law enforcement. Most students would probably stress why private security was needed and its emphasis on the prevention of crime rather than on the apprehension of criminals.

POSSIBLE ANSWERS TO THE DISCUSSION QUESTIONS

1. What features of ancient security systems may still be found in the 1990s?

   Features of ancient security systems still found in the 1990s include walls, locks and weapons as means of private protection.

2. Until recent times, it was felt a ruler and his army could enforce the laws. Why does Reith feel a "police mechanism" is necessary between the ruler and the army?

   Reith's main premise is that past civilizations fell because no police mechanism existed between the army of the ruler and the people. Without such a police mechanism to enforce the laws, the country fell into anarchy. When this occurred, armed troops were called in to restore order, but they secured only temporary relief. They were not a force that continuously remained in the community.

3. What relationship exists between the ancient assize of arms and our Constitution's Second Amendment right of the people "to keep and bear arms" for the necessity of a "well-regulated militia"?

   The Second Amendment probably evolved from the requirement that male citizens had to be armed to assist in policing the community.

4. Throughout history there has been hostility to the establishment of public police. Why were people so opposed to an organization that could have benefited them so greatly?

   Throughout history, people were opposed to establishment of public police because they feared it would result in tyranny. Since their actual experience was with armies and their abuses of individual freedom, people feared that establishing a police force would be like having a permanent army in their community.

5. In the absence of effective public law enforcement, what parallel functions did the Pinkerton Detective Agency and the railroad police perform?

   In the absence of public law enforcement, the Pinkerton Detective Agency and the railroad police functioned as the only national police force.

ANSWERS TO QUIZ 1

1.a, 2.b, 3.d, 4.d, 5.c, 6.b, 7.d, 8.c, 9.c, 10.a, 11.b, 12.a, 13.c, 14.c, 15.a, 16.b, 17.d, 18.d, 19.d, 20.a.

NOTES:

Notes, *continued*

Chapter 2

MODERN PRIVATE SECURITY: AN OVERVIEW

OBJECTIVES

Upon completing this chapter, the student will know:

- What private security is.
- What major functions are performed by private security officers.
- What the major types of private security personnel are.
- How proprietary private security differs from contractual private security.
- How private security services might be regulated.
- How private investigators/detectives are regulated.
- What the requirements for becoming a private investigator are.
- What a Certified Protection Profession (CPP) is.

KEY TERMS

The student will also be able to define the following terms: alarm respondent, armed courier services, armored car services, Certified Protection Professional (CPP), contract services, courier, guard, hybrid services, licensing, private security services, proprietary services, registration.

POSSIBLE RESPONSES TO THE APPLICATION

1. 1. Security officers are private police officers--FALSE. Security officers have a contractual obligation to whomever hires them to protect and secure a specific area or piece of property, yet they have no more authority to arrest than does an average citizen. Security officers' primary responsibility is "to observe and report . . . to call the correct authorities--such as the police or fire fighters--to handle the problem." However, in some cases, security officers may be sworn in as special police officers or deputy sheriffs with certain restrictive legal rights as foreseen by the agency authorizing public police authority.

2. The average security officer is a Rambo-like "wannabe cop"--FALSE. This is an image that labeled the private security officer during the strike-breaking days of the early 1900s. Today, security officers are commonly posted in hotel and condo buildings, in lobbies of high-rise office buildings, at industrial plants on nightwatch, in hospitals, malls and other public places where they act not only as security but also as information officers. Such work environments are hardly appealing to anyone with a Rambo mentality. A large percentage of those working as security officers are retirees seeking supplemental income, students working their way through school and homemakers.

3. Owners of security companies make huge profits from their low-paid labor force--FALSE. The business of providing security is very competitive. Today's security company is constantly struggling to provide better service at reduced costs. With increased insurance rates, costly equipment and increased salaries, many companies are just barely making a profit. Records of publicly-owned security companies (Pinkerton, Wackenhut) reveal annual net profit levels between one and three percent, a level significantly below most other industries. Such low profit levels prevent the raising of wages but also indicate that security companies are not getting rich at the expense of their employees.

4. All security officers dress like police, and most of them carry guns--FALSE. Many security officers wear sweaters or blazers, not formal-looking uniforms such as those worn by law enforcement officers. Although in some jurisdictions, the private security officer does dress similar to the public police officer, many laws have been passed by states stating differentials in uniforms. This has alleviated the problem of recognizing public police and private security officers. Most private security officers do not carry guns, due to liability and safety issues.

5. Private security officers are forever making unlawful arrests--FALSE. In general, security officers have no more authority to arrest than does the average citizen. Under certain emergency circumstances, when there is insufficient time to call the police, security officers may conduct a citizen's arrest. However, the number of arrests actually made by private security officers is very small compared to the number of officers in the field.

6. Security companies always fight any proposal that security officers all receive standardized training--FALSE. Top executives at most major contract security companies favor reformative efforts to improve the profession of private security. However, because of the wide variety of security jobs and the unique policies and procedures found at individual companies and industries, any attempt to provide in-depth standardized training for all security officers is likely to fall short for the requirements of a particular job site.

7. Few security officers stay on the job long. It's just a job to "pass through" to better things--FALSE. For many security officers, the job is a career. Some security officers stay on the job for twenty years and longer, while others "move on" after just a few years. Although the turnover for security officers is higher than for most other industries, much of this is due to the seasonal and temporary nature of many of the security jobs.

8. Most security officers are either stupid or have shady characters--FALSE. Security officers range in educational background from grammar school dropouts to PhD's, and only a small percentage are rejected for security employment following a background check. According to Tom Keating, Chairman of the Board at APS (American Protective

Services, Inc.): "The private security officer is one of the least understood, least appreciated and least compensated productive members of our society." Security work is very challenging, often involving long, late hours of solitude where the officer is expected to react to any situation which may suddenly arise. Security officers must also be able to make good judgment calls and construct clear and accurate reports.

2. Frequently the general public has a rather negative image of private security officers, believing them to be a step below public law enforcement officers. The emphasis on prevention of crime is seldom understood by the general public. Likewise, few lay persons are knowledgeable of the many restrictions imposed on private security officers. Unfortunately, this same lack of knowledge is often found among public law enforcement officers and sometimes even among individuals actively engaged in the private security field.

POSSIBLE ANSWERS TO THE DISCUSSION QUESTIONS

1. Is licensing of private security agencies and/or officers an advantage or disadvantage to private security agencies?

    Licensing usually means that performance standards have been established by a regulatory agency and, therefore, would be to the advantage of the agency. However, some states tend to place undue restrictions on private security agencies, making them non-competitive in the market.

2. Why is supervision so important to a private security agency?

    Supervision is important because an assortment of problems occur while performing the duties assigned to security officers. It is necessary to have a supervisor who has had a great deal of experience assist in providing adequate service to the employer. Usually supervision is stipulated as a responsibility in the contract to provide security services.

3. With or without specific regulations of private security officers in some states, what is the best way to ensure the maximum performance of these officers?

    With or without specific regulations of private security officers in some states, the best away to ensure the maximum performance of these officers is by establishing clear job descriptions and by adhering to a code of ethics that outlines the responsibilities of private security officers to enhance their image and to assure the professionalism of the industry.

4. Do you think private investigators enjoy more status than individuals in the private security work force?

    Whether private investigators enjoy more status than individuals in the private security work force is a matter of opinion. It usually becomes an attitude rather than a realistic issue. The television image of the private investigator certainly tends to elevate their status.

5. Consult your Yellow Pages. What security listings are given? Is there a listing for *polygraph services? Lie detection services? Surveillance?*

   Yellow Pages may have listings for both detective agencies and investigators. Which contains more listings will depend on the demand for services within a certain city or community. Larger cities tend to have greater demands, particularly where there is more crime. Conceivably, a city could have no listings.

SUGGESTED ACTIVITY

A key decision facing individuals entering the private security industry is whether to seek a position with a proprietary or a contractual security force. You might assign students to debate this topic, have two students role play why they feel proprietary/contractual is superior, or invite guest speakers representing both viewpoints to your class.

ANSWERS TO QUIZ 2

1.a, 2.c, 3.b, 4.b, 5.a, 6.b, 7.a, 8.c, 9.d, 10.a, 11.b, 12.d, 13.a, 14.b, 15.c, 16.c, 17.a, 18.d, 19.b, 20.d.

NOTES:

Chapter 3

THE PUBLIC/PRIVATE INTERFACE AND LEGAL AUTHORITY

OBJECTIVES

Upon completing this chapter, the student will know:

- How private security officers and public police officers are alike.
- How private security officers differ from public police officers.
- What authority private security officers have and how they are restricted.
- How private security officers compare in numbers with public police officers.
- How private and public security officers might work together.
- What advantages private security offers public police and vice versa.

KEY TERMS

The student will also be able to define the following terms: arrest, authority, Exclusionary Rule, POST commission, power, privatization.

POSSIBLE RESPONSE TO THE APPLICATION

1. The company might be hesitant to submit to the officers' request because it could increase the insurance rates of the Transit Commission. Whether the company should grant the officers' request to be sworn city reserve police officers or deputy sheriffs would depend a great deal on what types of attacks are occurring on the buses, who is doing the criminal activity and what the company's expectations were.

   Allowing the private security officers to be given special police officer or deputy sheriff status certainly would enhance their image aboard the buses, give the riders a more secure feeling and allow the officers more freedom in arresting possible perpetrators. It would also give the security officers an opportunity to work more closely with city police. The city police could train the private security officers on handling incidents aboard public transit buses.

POSSIBLE ANSWERS TO THE DISCUSSION QUESTIONS

1. What are the advantages and disadvantages of private security officers not being restricted by the U.S. Constitution (not having to give the Miranda warning, for instance)?

    Many legal scholars feel that because private security officers are normally working in the private sector they are not bound by constitutional issues. They feel only government agencies are bound by the Constitution. However, some courts feel very strongly that if private security is dealing in law enforcement activities they are bound by the Constitution. This seems to be a local issue. Courts are generally split as to what constraints ought to be placed upon private security officers. Officers should find out what the attitude of their local courts are.

2. How do private security officers assist public police officers in your community? Vice versa?

    Answers will vary by community. In most instances there is a very close working relationship with the public police, particularly in crime prevention activities and reporting to the public police possible suspicious criminal activity as viewed by a private security officer.

3. Should the private police be trained by the public police in some aspects of handling unruly individuals? Discuss both the positive and negative aspects of such training.

    In some cases private security officer are given personal defensive training on how to protect themselves from unruly persons However, this is unofficial. Most large private security companies have their own training departments which train their personnel. To officially allow public police to train private security officers gets into an area of liability, insurance and tort actions. Most public agencies will not train private security officers.

4. Do you feel police officers should be allowed to moonlight as private security providers? Why or why not?

    Some police administrators feel that moonlighting interferes with the officer's performance on their public police job. Private security says police officers take away jobs from others when they moonlight. Business and industry want the authority of the uniform on their premises. Many different opinions exist on this controversial subject.

5. Who do you feel has more status, private or public officers? Why? Do you foresee a change in status for either group in the future?

    Change in status comes slowly in a democracy. The public police are under constant criticism regarding police brutality, while the private security officer is under constant criticism because of lack of sufficient training. Historically, public police have enjoyed higher status, but this is changing as private policing becomes professionalized.

ANSWERS TO QUIZ 3

1.b, 2.b, 3.d, 4.d, 5.c, 6.d, 7.b, 8.d, 9.d, 10.b, 11.d, 12.b, 13.d, 14.a, 15.b, 16.a, 17.d, 18.b, 19.d, 20.d.

NOTES:

Notes, *continued*

Chapter 4

LEGAL LIABILITY

OBJECTIVES

Upon completing this chapter, the student will know:

- How laws may be classified.
- How a crime differs from a tort.
- What a tort is.
- What a nondelegable duty is.
- How civil law is further categorized.
- What the elements of negligent liability are.
- For what actions security officers are most frequently sued.
- What Section 1983 of the United States Code, Title 43, the Civil Rights Act, establishes and how it might affect private security.
- How civil liability can be reduced.
- What the Six-Layered Liability Protection System includes.

KEY TERMS

The student will also be able to define the following terms: armed personnel, assault, battery, civil liability, civil offense, collective deep pocket, crime, criminal offense, defamation, deposition, excessive force, false imprisonment, foreseeable danger, intentional infliction of emotional distress, intentional wrong, interrogatories, invasion of privacy, negligence, nondelegable duty, plaintiff, precedents, proximate result, punitive damages, reasonable care, respondent superior, restitution, Section 1983, strict liability, substantive damages, tort, vicarious liability.

POSSIBLE RESPONSES TO THE APPLICATION

1. Certainly there are precedent cases to resolve this particular litigation. By contracting with the business to provide security services, the security guard creates a special relationship between himself and the tenant's lessee. The question of duty in this case might be for a jury to decide, inasmuch as we do not know what the responsibilities of the security officers were. Were they required to patrol each floor? If so, how often? Why wasn't someone at the post when Mrs. Grambling came into the office complex? These are unresolved questions. Negligence would have to be determined by a jury based on additional facts.

2. To protect herself fully, she should have notified the post she was in her office. However, because nobody was present when she entered the building, it is difficult to say if a jury would admonish her for her actions. She assumed that no one was on duty, and we all make assumptions everyday on what we see and hear.

3. The first thing that comes to mind, without a jury trial, is that the Mid-Atlantic Security Company could be 90% negligent in that the post they were responsible for was vacated. Estelle Grambling might be 10% responsible for not attempting to contact the post officers after she entered her office. It is difficult to second-guess juries.

4. An interesting discussion could ensue with the various opinions of the students.

POSSIBLE ANSWERS TO THE DISCUSSION QUESTIONS

1. Liability is often used to refer to a person failing to do something he or she should have. What does that really mean in general terms?

   The word *liability* is a broad legal term of the most comprehensive significance, including almost every character of hazard or responsibility. There is absolute liability, fixed liability, joint liability and many other types, too numerous to mention. There is liability created by statute, liability insurance, liability limits and liability imposed by law. To gain a better perspective of the legal definition of liability, students are encouraged to look up its meaning in Black's Law Dictionary, available in most libraries.

2. There is a continuous ravaging of the Old English common law principle that the master is not responsible for the criminal acts of his servants. Explain what this actually means as far as legal liability is concerned.

   The relation of master and servant exists where one person, for pay or other valuable consideration, enters into the service of another, devoting personal labor for an agreed period. In this case it is assumed that a private security officer who falters in his duties and damages a third party would expose his employer and contractor to legal litigation. Courts are increasingly finding the contractor of private security services more and more guilty of a portion of the liability.

3. As a security officer, do you believe in the theory of foreseeable danger?

   Foreseeable danger is quite a controversial issue. Courts are leaning away from the theory of foreseeable danger as a defense, believing that a first-time victim would suffer immeasurable harm in a lawsuit where no foreseeable danger was present. In such a case, where no previous crime has been committed prior to the victim's experience, allowing foreseeable danger as a defense would have an adverse effect on the victim's lawsuit.

4. What is your understanding of punitive damages?

   Punitive damages are also known as exemplary damages. They are usually awarded to a plaintiff over and above the compensation for the loss and are given to punish the defendant and to set an example for similar wrongdoers. Some states have laws against punitive damages in certain types of cases and courts have been reluctant to award punitive damages in private security cases.

5. Why do the public police favor the private security sector handling economic crimes?

   Public police feel that economic crimes can be better handled by the private sector because they consume too much investigative time, are usually non-productive when it comes to setting an example of crime prevention and usually occur over a long period of time. Others feel the public police lack the training and personnel to undertake the overwhelming problems existing as a result of economic crimes. In one area alone, the misuse of computers is rampant with very little enforcement because of a lack of expertise in the field. Public police feel that their time can be more effective serving the public in other threatening areas. Also there is the factor that those who are victims of economic crimes are more interested in restitution than they are in prosecuting a suspect.

ANSWERS TO QUIZ 4

1.c, 2.d, 3.a, 4.b, 5.a, 6.c, 7.d, 8.c, 9.d, 10.d, 11.b, 12.c, 13.a, 14.d, 15.d, 16.a, 17.b, 18.a, 19.c, 20.c.

NOTES:

Notes, *continued*

Chapter 5

ENHANCING SECURITY THROUGH PHYSICAL CONTROLS

OBJECTIVES

Upon completing this chapter, the student will know:

- What four purposes are served by physical controls.
- What three lines of defense are important in physical security.
- How the perimeter, the exterior and the interior of a facility can be made more secure.
- What the two common types of safes are and why the distinction is important.
- What constitutes basic security equipment.
- What kinds of locks are available and what type of key lock is recommended.
- What functions are performed by lighting.
- What the components of a total lighting system are.
- What types of alarms are available for the three lines of defense.
- Where alarms may be received.
- What factors must be balanced in selecting physical controls.
- What two factors are critical in establishing and maintaining physical controls.

KEY TERMS

The student will also be able to define the following terms: area alarms, biometric, capacity alarms, central station alarms, concertina, crash bar, crime prevention through environmental design (CPTED), cylindrical locks, dead bolts, envelope (building), exculpatory clauses, fail-safe locks, fail-secure locks, fenestration, fiber optic, header, keyway, local alarms, luminaire, panic bar, perimeter alarms, perimeter barriers, point alarms, police-connected alarm, proprietary alarms, razor ribbon, safe, slipping (a lock), space alarms, spot alarms, spring-loaded bolts, strike, telephone dialer, top guard, vault, warded locks, watchclock.

POSSIBLE RESPONSES TO THE APPLICATION

1. Evaluating a lighting system's energy efficiency requires considering many more features than just the energy efficiency of lamps (light bulbs and tubes). Ballasts, luminaires (fixtures), controls, operating practices and maintenance are several factors to consider.

   The first element to consider is the efficiency of the lamps. According to the American Society for Industrial Security (ASIS), installing high-efficiency fluorescent tubes can result in an immediate energy and operating cost savings of 14%. Relatively minor system-oriented modifications can result in a 52% energy savings and a 54% annual cost savings--certainly worth considering.

   One such system modification is to replace ballasts with new, high-efficiency ballasts that reduce energy consumption without an accompanying loss of light. Using both high-efficiency lamps and ballasts can reduce energy use by up to 20% without reducing the amount of light.

   Another factor to consider is how and when the lights are used. Employees should be reminded to turn out lights that are not needed. Sometimes, however, lighting systems do not allow this because several lights are all controlled by a single circuit breaker. All have to be on when perhaps only half are needed. Likewise, few lighting system have a dimming capability. They must be used at full power even when less is required. Improved switching and automatic controls such as time clocks, dimmers and photocells not only reduce waste, they also increase the lighting system's usefulness and flexibility.

   Another factor to consider is maintenance of the lighting system. The usual practice is to replace lamps when they burn out. Such "spot relamping" is very wasteful because lamps' efficiency declines with use. It is generally more cost effective to replace all the lamps in a large area <u>before</u> they burn out. According to the ASIS, this method, called "group relamping," can save about ninety cents on each spot relamping dollar spent. Group relamping also allows use of contract lighting maintenance, providing even more savings.

   The ASIS stresses that many other factors can affect the overall lighting system's efficiency, including how the luminaires are laid out in relationship to the area they illuminate, the lenses and louvers (shielding or diffusing media) used in luminaires and environmental conditions such as heat, humidity and dust. Additional considerations are the interrelationships between different lighting system components (including daylighting) and the interrelationships between the lighting system and other systems in the building such as heating, ventilating and air conditioning.

2. This application can be done individually, as a group project or as a class project. Answers to security problems will vary with individuals as to what provides the ultimate in security. Cost factors and budgetary constraints may cause inadequate equipment to be installed, consequently causing problems.

3. Answers will depend upon local circumstances.

POSSIBLE ANSWERS TO THE DISCUSSION QUESTIONS

1. Most adults have several keys in their possession. How many keys are in your possession? What types of locks do they fit? Compare the different types of keys that others have with your own.

   Most individuals will have in their possession a minimum of three keys: two automobile keys and a house key. However, many people have numerous other keys, fitting locks that protect overnight cases, suitcases, briefcases, lockers, freezers, buildings, offices, safety deposit boxes, dispensing machines and the like. The shapes, sizes and uses of various keys for various locks is unending.

2. Local communities frequently pass ordinances to curtail false-alarm responses by the public police. From the user's standpoint, is this an advantage or a disadvantage?

   As a result of certain ordinances curtailing false alarms, users often have been discouraged and, in too many cases, have rendered the system useless by deactivating it. Fines assessed for false alarms that are beyond the user's control have placed both installers and users at odds with local officials. For example, in some cases lightning and storms have inadvertently set off an alarm system, yet the owners were fined. Many owners and installers feel government officials are uncompromisingly intolerant of false alarms.

3. Despite the numerous advantages offered by a reliable surveillance system, what disadvantages might be expected?

   Reliable surveillance systems are expensive and sometimes inadequately provide the necessary security originally expected. To be effective, closed circuit television monitors must have an individual to watch the sets constantly. This presents a problems not only because personnel costs are continually rising, but also because finding competent personnel is becoming increasingly difficult.

4. Security managers frequently overcompensate in protecting areas with fencing. List some guidelines you would consider before recommending any type of outside security fencing.

   A security manager might consider environmental security planning and design processes before recommending any type of outside security fencing. Fencing represents the securing of a building so outsiders cannot gain access without authorization. This view has gained widespread acceptance because of its practicality and seemingly immediate results. Implicit with the fencing approach is the idea that the place to be protected is defensible. Besides the social costs of a fortress model, the dollar costs of security personnel might be such that few businesses or industries could afford security fencing.

5. In providing for security needs, why are aesthetics important to the security manager?

   Lack of good aesthetics in security planning may actually generate more anxiety for people by presenting a fearful image of potential danger, such as the excessive presence of armed, uniformed security guards and extensive protection equipment. It is important that the physical surroundings not display a hostile environment to those who are exposed daily to the physical design.

ADDITIONAL INFORMATION

The value of alarm systems to police agencies, the courts and the taxpayer has not been fully realized. Alarm systems free up police resources, allowing public police officers to spend more time in areas with high crime rates and with fewer premises protected by alarm systems. Police may also devote more manpower to apprehending criminals. In this way, the police and alarm companies can work together, complementing each other as they wage a mutual war on crime.

Alarm systems afford further savings in the costs of investigating and prosecuting criminals. When an alarm signal enables police to apprehend a suspect on the scene, the investigation is greatly simplified and a conviction is almost certain. In such cases, investigatory work becomes a formality as the police are eyewitnesses. Usually the criminal's only hope is to plea-bargain a reduced sentence. Consequently, the trial progresses swiftly and court costs are reduced across the board. One fact is certain: those thousands of alarm arrests have saved the courts and detectives considerable time and the tax-paying public millions of dollars.

Although alarm systems have become increasingly sophisticated, they do not necessarily have to be so. Dogs are frequently used as relatively inexpensive "alarms." Much less commonly used, but equally effective, are geese. For example, geese have been used for 15 years at the Ballantine Scotch Distillery in Scotland to protect the perimeter from outside intruders. The geese wander around the entire distillery which is fenced in and has only one guard for the whole complex. If an intruder tries to scale the fence or to enter the premises illegally, the geese put up a tremendous holler that brings the guard to investigate. This also gives the guard ample warning so that he can call the public police.

ANSWERS TO QUIZ 5

1.d, 2.a, 3.d, 4.b, 5.c, 6.c, 7.a, 8.c, 9.b, 10.a, 11.d, 12.c, 13.a, 14.b, 15.b, 16.b, 17.c, 18.d, 19.d, 20.a.

NOTES:

Chapter 6

ENHANCING SECURITY THROUGH PROCEDURAL CONTROLS

OBJECTIVES

Upon completing this chapter, the student will know:

- What shrinkage is.
- What hiring procedures can help reduce shrinkage and negligence lawsuits.
- What educational measures can help promote security.
- How most procedural controls seek to prevent loss.
- What specific procedures can be used to control access to an area.
- What characterizes an effective employee badge or pass.
- What constitutes effective key control.
- What an effective closing procedure ensures.
- When opening and closing is a two-person operation.
- What areas are particularly vulnerable to theft.
- What accounting procedures can help prevent shrinkage.
- What procedures can help detect theft or pilferage.
- When searches of lockers, vehicles, packages and persons are acceptable.
- What procedures to use when transporting valuables.
- What additional protection against financial loss is available to owners/managers.

KEY TERMS

The student will also be able to define the following terms: blind receiving, change key, employment records, fidelity bonds, grand master key, integrity interview, master key, master keying system, neuter head blank, perpetual inventory, polygraph, shrinkage, sub-master key.

POSSIBLE RESPONSE TO THE APPLICATION

The "Preventing Employee Pilferage" rules should be evaluated according to what type of business or industrial complex a security manager is responsible for. Students might be assigned to such areas as wholesaling, manufacturing, retailing, and distributing and asked to match the rules with existing prevalent dishonest practices.

POSSIBLE ANSWERS TO THE DISCUSSION QUESTIONS

1. Why is curbing pilferage so important to a security manager?

    Curbing pilferage is important because the pilferer is the number one problem in most businesses. While most people believe that shoplifting and external theft bring the heaviest losses, employee dishonesty is by far the greatest source of loss, and the cumulative effect is substantial. A recent study of corporate bankruptcies showed that almost half of these were in some way related to employee theft.

2. What factual information should be obtained to make the decision to employ or not to employee an applicant?

    Important information to obtain when making employment decisions includes the applicant's past employment history, present and past residences, personal reputation and family life, credit and community standings, education, social affiliations, business connections, record of criminal conviction and/or civil suits and pertinent job-related information.

3. What procedures can be used regarding employee coats, purses and packages to deter internal theft?

    To deter internal theft, store employees' coats, purses, and packages away from the selling floor. If possible, provide lockers to secure the employees' valuables and clothing. If lockers are not provided, establish some procedures to get and secure employees' packages and personal belongings until the employees are ready to leave work. Unfortunately, most stores were not designed with physical security controls in mind. It may be necessary to spot-check the employees as they leave the store to determine if the packages they are carrying contain stolen merchandise.

4. What are some rationales frequently given by employees for stealing from their employers?

    Included among the rationales frequently given by employees for stealing from their employers are: They owe it to me. They have it coming to them. I need it more than they do. They'll never miss it. Everybody else does it. Causes of employee dishonesty usually fall into two groups: (1) a psychological environment conducive to employee embezzlement and (2) opportunities that, in reality, are invitations to steal.

5. What employee actions might lead security personnel to suspect dishonesty?

Many employee actions might lead security personnel to suspect dishonesty. Complaining of debt is one such action. Employees is debt are generally easily recognized. The deeper in debt the employees are, the more likely they are to steal, particularly if they are in a position that offers the opportunity to steal. Closely related to this is domestic problems. Divorce or separation can put an employee into financial difficulty. This is not to say that every employee who goes through divorce or separation is going to steal, but people with domestic problems bear watching. Lack of pride should also be a signal to security managers. Employees who lack pride in their work seldom communicate respect for their employers. Such people will steal from the company with little reason and think nothing of it. Tardiness is another action bearing watching. While not conclusive, lack of punctuality can be indicative of problems because employees who steal time may steal other things if given the opportunity. Perhaps the most obvious action is someone living beyond his or her means. Thousands of employees have been caught stealing from their companies when it was discovered that their spending habits were well beyond their income.

ADDITIONAL INFORMATION

Among the most important procedural controls are hiring procedures. This is especially true when security personnel are being hired. Before a manager commits to hiring an individual whose background indicates that he or she would qualify, several other factors must be considered. Among them are the person's age and that of his or her subordinates, whether that individual would follow a logical career path entering into the position, the person's ability to communicate effectively and to relate effectively to the work environment. Consideration should also be given to the person's intelligence and whether the job would be challenging to the individual. Further, it is important to note the individual's values. Would the job fulfill certain needs for money, power, knowledge, aesthetics and social good? Special considerations, such as does the person have a unique reputation that might benefit the organization, may also exist.

ANSWERS TO QUIZ 6

1.a, 2.c, 3.d, 4.d, 5.c, 6.d, 7.a, 8.b, 9.d, 10.d, 11.b, 12.c, 13.a, 14.a, 15.d, 16.d, 17.c, 18.b, 19.c, 20.d.

NOTES:

Notes, *continued*

Chapter 7

PREVENTING LOSSES FROM ACCIDENTS AND EMERGENCIES

OBJECTIVES

Upon completing this chapter, the student will know:

- Why accident prevention is often part of a security manager's responsibility.
- What OSHA is and how it relates to private security as well as what records it requires.
- What causes the vast majority of accidents and how they can be prevented or reduced.
- What the security manager's role is during civil disturbances, riots and strikes.
- What the primary defenses against bombs are.
- How a bomb threat can be prepared for, received and acted on.
- What three elements are required for a fire to occur.
- How fires are classified.
- How fires can be prevented.
- What equipment can help protect lives and assets from fire.
- What types of fire detectors are available.
- When water or a Class A fire extinguisher should *not* be used.
- What procedures help protect against loss by fire.
- What the security manager's responsibilities are in the event of a fire.
- What natural disaster plans should be formulated.

KEY TERMS

The student will also be able to define the following terms: fire-loading, fire triangle, ignition temperature, infrared detectors, ionization detectors, Occupational Safety and Health Administration (OSHA), Occupational Safety and Health Act, photoelectric detectors, thermal detectors.

POSSIBLE RESPONSE TO THE APPLICATION

The emergency procedures established for the college faculty should be effective in the areas covered. The procedures are clear, concise and leave little doubt as to what is to be done, when and by whom.

POSSIBLE ANSWERS TO THE DISCUSSION QUESTIONS

1. What alternatives are available to security managers in handling personnel conflicts? Are they the responsibility of the security manager?

   From time to time security managers must alleviate an inflamed situation where workers, union or non-union, may disrupt the establishment's daily routine. In such situations, the security officers must maintain a neutral attitude and rely either on the establishment's policy or that of the contract agency for whom they work. Security officers are responsible not only for preventing losses, but also for quelling any outbreaks until those in charge can rectify the situation.

2. What natural disasters are likely to occur in your geographic area, and how should a security manager prepare for an adequate response to them?

   Natural disasters such as flooding and violent storms are most prevalent in certain parts of the country, and continuous planning then becomes a matter of routine. However, when fire, explosions or riots have been known to occur, many industries and businesses have inadequate planning to cope with such disasters. The time to prepare is before the occurrence. A well-defined plan that is updated continuously is an asset to the organization and will prove its worth should any natural disaster occur.

3. What resources would you contact to counter a series of bomb threats against your facility?

   The best resource to contact to counter a series a bomb threats is the local police department. Where army ordinance units are stationed, they, too, could be of value.

4. When a strike is certain to occur, what contingency plans should a security manager be concerned about?

   If a strike is certain to occur, plans should be made for the possibility of violence against persons and property. A well-designed strike plan will pay dividends in preventing assaults and the deliberate destruction of company property. Local police departments often will assist and provide resources to curb such deviant activity.

5. If a security director notices OSHA violations and reports them to top management, and top management chooses to ignore the violations, what should the security director do?

Security directors must abide by management policies regarding OSHA violations. It is the director's responsibility to bring any violations to management's attention, but correcting these violations may be someone else's responsibility.

ADDITIONAL INFORMATION

Private security officers should be informed of any emergency plan they might have to implement. Of utmost important is the type of emergency that might occur. Security officers must be familiar with any available maps, procedural charts or call-up lists and must have available a listing of local resource that might be needed.

Every emergency plan should have a designated control center. This center should offer some protection from the effects of the ongoing emergency or from the effects of natural disasters such as explosions, tornadoes and the like. An emergency operating center or control center must also be a communication center so that responsible officials gathered there can be kept informed of the developing situation and can base control decisions on factual information.

No one communications system is ideal for coping with all disasters. The most practical approach is to make an inventory of all existing communications systems in the affected areas and to then determine how they can be tied in with each other and with communications systems within the community for emergency purposes. Most important, all emergency actions should have centralized coordination.

ANSWERS TO QUIZ 7

1.a, 2.d, 3.c, 4.d, 5.a, 6.c, 7.b, 8.c, 9.b, 10.a, 11.b, 12.c, 13.d, 14.d, 15.c, 16. answers will vary, 17.a, 18.d, 19.b, 20.c.

NOTES:

Notes, *continued*

Chapter 8

PREVENTING LOSSES FROM CRIMINAL ACTIONS

OBJECTIVES

Upon completing this chapter, the student will know:

- How criminal and civil offenses differ.
- What crimes are of major importance to private security.
- How the risk of these crimes can be reduced.
- How to differentiate among theft, burglary and robbery.
- What circumstances can indicate arson.
- What white-collar crime is.
- What pilferage is.
- What drugs are commonly abused in the workplace.
- What rights private security officers may be called on to enforce.
- When and how private security officers can make an arrest.
- When force or deadly force may be justified.
- When and how searches of suspects can be conducted.
- How interviewing differs from interrogating, as well as how to make such questioning more effective.

KEY TERMS

The student will also be able to define the following terms: arson, assault, burglary, citizen's arrest, civil offenses, cocaine, corporate crime, crack, economic crime, embezzlement, felony, fraud, freebase, grand larceny, igniter, interrogation, interview, larceny/theft, marijuana, misdemeanor, petty larceny, pilferage, pyromaniac, robbery, torts, trespassing, trailers, Uniform Crime Reports (UCR), unlawful taking, vandalism, white-collar crime.

30 Chapter 8

POSSIBLE RESPONSES TO THE APPLICATION

1. Officer Ross did an excellent job with prompt, efficient action. Her alertness, the gathering of evidence and her promptness in turning over the youngsters to the public police reflect a high level of competence and professionalism.

2. This incident involves a simple theft rather than a robbery because of the absence of any threat to do bodily harm. The security manager would use pre-established company policy as a guideline for further action. The suspect might simply be turned over to the police. Or the security manager might have the responsibility of taking a statement from the witness and then turning the suspect over to the police. Or it could be that the company has a non-involvement policy and no action would be taken to prosecute Myers.

3. Again, company policy would determine the course of action to take. At this point the security director does not know whether anything is missing from the safe or not. If money or valuable documents are missing, most company guidelines establish that the public police are called to conduct a crime scene search and then investigate the burglary. The primary role of the security director is to protect the crime scene until the public police arrive, to answer their questions and to then attempt to determine how security was broken (not who broke it) so that corrective action can be taken.

4. Answers will vary for this application.

POSSIBLE ANSWERS TO THE DISCUSSION QUESTIONS

1. Private security officers are sometimes asked to arrest people. As a security director, what policies or guidelines would you adopt to cover these situations?

    Guidelines or policies related to arresting people should be developed with the advice of the legal department. The type of business one is engaged in and the type of property being stolen will dictate what policies should be made. A different set of policies should be established for handling juveniles and for handling adults. It is also advisable to contact the local police department for guidance in establishing such guidelines.

2. Discuss the advantages and disadvantages of private security officers carrying firearms.

    The advantages and disadvantages of private security officers carrying firearms will vary with the type of assignment the officer has. Responsibility for guarding valuables such as diamonds, paintings, large sums of money, gold, silver or V.I.P.s certainly justifies carrying a weapon. However, many disadvantages occur where marginal justification exists, such as patrolling residential areas, office complexes or industrial plants where no obvious threat exists.

3. What differences exist between interviewing a witness and interrogating a suspect?

    When people are interviewed, it is usually for the specific purpose of obtaining information from the victim of or witness to a crime. Such individuals are more likely to be cooperative than persons who are suspected of being involved in the crime. An interrogation of suspects is aimed at obtaining information to implicate the suspects; consequently, they are unlikely to be cooperative. This necessitates different questioning techniques to obtain the required information.

4. Compare the statutory arrest authority of private citizens (Table 8-2) with those of public police officers in your state. How do the arrest powers of private security officers compare with those of public police officers in your state?

   The statutory arrest authority of private citizens, public police officers and private security officers varies from state to state. Refer to the tables in this chapter as well as to Appendix A.

5. Why are some crimes divided into categories or degrees?

   Crimes are divided into categories or degrees because legislatures pass laws that must be arbitrary. Yet the amount of loss or harm caused varies from offense to offense. Consequently, legislatures establish different levels with an accompanying type of punishment for each of the more common, frequently committed types of crimes such as larceny/theft, burglary, robbery and murder.

ADDITIONAL INFORMATION

Whether security officers must give suspects the Miranda Warning prior to questioning them is often the subject of dispute. The following cases might provide the basis for an interesting class discussion of this topic.

Six private security officers employed by a New York department store detained a store employee and interrogated her in connection with suspected shoplifting. They did not give the Miranda Warning, and the court did not require that they should have done so. The court stated that the Miranda rule applied only to law enforcement officers. There was no indication that the officers acted upon the direction or request of public law enforcement officers [*People v. Frank*, 52 Misc. 2d 266, 275 N.Y.S. 2d 570 (Sup. Ct. N.Y., 1966)].

A security officer employed at a county hospital, owned and operated by a governmental agency in California, was held not to be a law enforcement officer within the meaning of Miranda. The court stated that the term "authorities" as used in Miranda meant a peace officer employed by an agency of the government whose chief function was the enforcement of the law (*People v. Wright*, 249 Cal. App. 2d 692, 57 Cal. Rptr. 781, 1967).

The overwhelming weight of authority has now firmly established that the pre-interrogation warnings found in Miranda have a bearing upon the rights of the accused only if the condition of custodial interrogation by law enforcement authorities exists. There is no need to advise accused suspects of their Miranda rights unless all three precedent conditions are discoverable in the facts of the case: (1) custody, (2) interrogation and (3) presence of a law enforcement interrogator (*State v. Bolan*, 27 Ohio St. 2d 15, 271 N.E. 2d 839, 1971).

While much of the case law succeeding the landmark decision of *Miranda v. Arizona* has struggled with the terms "custody" and "interrogation," most courts to date have found little difficulty in deciding who is <u>not</u> a law enforcement officer.

ANSWERS TO QUIZ 8

1.b, 2.a, 3.a, 4.c, 5.d, 6.b, 7.b, 8.d, 9.c, 10.b, 11.a, 12.d, 13.d, 14.c, 15.c, 16.b, 17.a, 18.c, 19.b, 20.a.

NOTES:

Chapter 9

ENHANCING INFORMATION/COMPUTER SECURITY

OBJECTIVES

Upon completing this chapter, the student will know:

- How valuable proprietary information may be obtained by competitors or criminals.
- Whether trash can be legally searched by others.
- What telecommunications security involves.
- What constitutes computer crime.
- How serious computer crime is.
- What the greatest threats to computer centers are.
- What legislation pertains to computer crime.
- What security measures can be taken to reduce losses from computer crime.
- What factors to consider when investigating a computer crime.
- Who the typical "electronic criminal" is.
- What the probability of detection of computer crimes and the risk of prosecution are.

KEY TERMS

The student will also be able to define the following terms: check kiting, computer crime, computer virus, cyberspace, encryption, facsimile, faxpionage, hacker, industrial espionage, noncompete agreements, nondisclosure agreements, OPSEC, secrecy agreements, telecommunications, virtual corporation, virus.

POSSIBLE RESPONSES TO THE APPLICATION

1. a. It is not likely unless he had the access code. The crime would be forgery.

   b. It is even less likely that he could break into the Defense Department's secret computer. The crime involved would depend on what he did once he gained access. It could be theft, sabotage or espionage.

2. a. The formal charge would be theft by forgery.

   b. The suspect would be located through credit bureaus, banks and perhaps use of an investigator/detective agency.

   c. Nicholson could sue Nickolson for mental anguish.

POSSIBLE ANSWERS TO THE DISCUSSION QUESTIONS

1. How familiar are you with computer systems? Which specific types?

   Many students may not be familiar with computer systems or specific types. Exposure to these will depend on varied circumstances. Students not familiar are encouraged to try to find a resource that might be available for this type of knowledge.

2. Have there been recent computer crimes in your area? If so, what did they involve?

   Students must realize that information regarding computer crime is hard to come by because business and industry want protection from publicity. It is only when an occasional hacker comes to the attention of the press that knowledge of computer crime comes to life.

3. Do you know any computer hackers (or are you one yourself)? What types of activities are they most interested in? Do they perceive anything illegal about their activities?

   Knowledge and opinions about computer hackers will vary. Discussion should be confined to actual knowledge and reported cases only.

4. How reliant is your local bank on a computer system?

   To find out how much your local bank relies on a computer system, contact a bank officer. He or she, however, might be reluctant to give out corporate information.

5. Do you feel penalties for hackers should be as severe as they are under the Electronic Communications Privacy Act of 1986?

   Whether students feel penalties for hackers should be as severe as they are under the Electronic Communication Privacy Act of 1986 will vary according to individual ideas, attitudes and direct knowledge.

ADDITIONAL INFORMATION

Industry and business today, because of their huge financial investments and their need for a comprehensive protection plan for both physical and computer data, are calling upon private security agencies for assistance. Computers are vulnerable to many problems, including fire, flood, sabotage, operator error, simple carelessness, theft of information, programming fraud and embezzlement. With the lack of security, computer-related crimes are becoming more and more prevalent. To comply with the demand for services in computer security, private security agencies must develop data security training programs so material and techniques that lead to maximum protection can be developed, organized and distributed. There is a growing need for expanding training programs and hiring competent professionals who can satisfy a client's needs.

ANSWERS TO QUIZ 9

1.b, 2.c, 3.d, 4.d, 5.d, 6.c, 7.d, 8.b, 9.d, 10.b, 11.d, 12.b, 13.c, 14.a, 15.b, 16.b, 17.a, 18.d, 19.c, 20.d.

NOTES:

Notes, *continued*

Chapter 10

ENHANCING PUBLIC RELATIONS

OBJECTIVES

Upon completing this chapter, the student will know:

- What public relations is.
- What role security personnel have in public relations.
- What factors are important to effective public relations.
- What special populations security personnel must learn to interact with.
- What medical or other conditions can be mistaken for intoxication or being high on drugs.
- What balance security managers should strive for when dealing with the press and the media.
- How effective public relations affects security.

KEY TERMS

The student will also be able to define the following terms: Alzheimer's disease (A.D.), disability, epilepsy, public relations.

POSSIBLE RESPONSE TO THE APPLICATION

Private security personnel might play a role in any of the public relations efforts listed and many others as well.

POSSIBLE ANSWERS TO THE DISCUSSION QUESTIONS

1. What type of uniform would you prefer to wear and why?

    Most private security officers would prefer to wear a uniform that identifies them as closely as possible to public police officers. Recognizing the visual items that cause the public to mistake private security personnel for law enforcement officers, many cities have adopted ordinances and state laws regulating the use of colors, insignias, badges and vehicles of contractual private security agencies. Recently these laws have also included proprietary agencies. Enforcing these laws is usually handled by the state or local police. Security managers usually prefer to dress as business executives.

2. In what types of businesses is public relations most important?

    Any business that deals with the public directly must consider public relations a necessity. Public relations enhances the agency's image, develops business and informs the public of the business's goals and objectives.

3. Why is a sense of humor important for security personnel?

    In a world fraught with problems, suspicions and lack of trust, a sense of humor can temper a situation that could otherwise be explosive. Although private security is a serious business, interjecting humor where appropriate may prevent what otherwise might become a negative situation.

4. Why are communication skills important for security personnel?

    Communication skills are critical to security personnel. When you think of communications, you often think of radios, alarm equipment, criminal justice information systems and digital systems. You do not frequently think of verbal communications which requires security personnel to inform and convey information to someone else. Effective verbal communication between security personnel and the public helps the public understand what security is about. The public's attitude toward and acceptance of security often is formulated as the result of the information they receive from an officer. Some segments of society have little confidence in what they know and see. This usually develops into total misunderstanding of private security. The private security officer's knowledge and communication skills can prevent this.

5. What activities might a security officer volunteer to do to promote public relations?

    Security officers or managers might volunteer for several activities to promote public relations, such as those listed in the Application. Personal contact with the public they serve shapes the image of the private security agency. A well-informed security professional, who is engaged in communication activities, is in a position to enhance his or her agency's image.

ADDITIONAL INFORMATION

All private security agencies, whether contractual or proprietary, should evaluate their communication with the employers they serve. Only through two-way communication will the needs and expectations of the employer be known. In addition, every private security officer should have sufficient information about the organization to answer questions regarding its policies. When an employer hires a private security agency, the agency is part of the company, not apart from it. Private security officers must learn how to cooperate with the employer and establish effective communication. This will enhance the trust and confidence the employer has in the agency and enhance the attitude of the employees. Private security agencies should be responsive to the recommendations of the employer and must weigh the wants and needs of the agency in relationship to the demands of the employer. Good public relations fosters additional business and open communications.

ANSWERS TO QUIZ 10

1.a, 2.a, 3.d, 4.d, 5.a, 6.b, 7.b, 8.d, 9.b, 10.c, 11.b, 12.d, 13.d, 14.d, 15.a, 16.d, 17.d, 18.c, 19.d, 20.a.

NOTES:

Notes, *continued*

Chapter 11

THE INVESTIGATIVE FUNCTION

OBJECTIVES

Upon completing this chapter, the student will know:

- What a primary characteristic of an effective investigator is.
- What the primary responsibilities of an investigator are.
- What questions investigators must seek answers to.
- What the single most important factor is in the successful disposition of an incident.
- What makes sexual harassment illegal.
- What must be present before security officers can begin a criminal investigation.
- What crimes security personnel are likely to be asked to investigate.

KEY TERMS

The student will also be able to define the following terms: cybercop, investigate, predication.

POSSIBLE RESPONSE TO THE APPLICATION

In this case, it is helpful that Bart Gibson is an employee of the company. Had he not been, it would have complicated matters to the extent of an unknown quantity would have been introduced to the case.

As in most conspiracies, there are always those who will want to make a deal to save themselves. In this case, whether Gary is worth dealing with is questionable. First it has to be determined what is company policy in a case like this. Therefore, management must be apprised of the situation first. It is their attitude that will determine whether Bart Gibson and his security director should continue the investigation or whether it should be turned over to the public police. It must be that a joint investigative effort should be instituted inasmuch as there is an outside resource of stolen property involved.

Questions such as what effect this will have on other employees should be addressed. There is one positive note that an investigator should keep in mind in this type of case. Make no promises. Stating you will do all you can to assist the perpetrator is sufficient. After all, you are dealing with someone who is a thief.

POSSIBLE ANSWERS TO THE DISCUSSION QUESTIONS

1. How would you go about obtaining the basic skills needed to become an effective investigator?

   The basic skills needed to become an effective investigator usually requires that the person take classroom studies to acquire a fundamental background to investigations. A balance must be obtained through acquired study, experience and the artful application of learned techniques.

2. What resources would you use if you were involved in a financial investigation?

   Because financial investigations are not very frequent, the investigator must usually rely upon experts in the fields of computers, accounting and auditing. On-line and CD-ROM database searches are especially helpful to locate, verify and identify investigations and to obtain background information in most financial investigations.

3. What do you feel is the most important factor in determining the successful disposition of an incident you investigated?

   Satisfying the client or the company that you are working for is perhaps the most important factor. If the investigation comes to a successful conclusion with an outcome that is acceptable to the client in every way, then this becomes a successful disposition, whether property is recovered, a criminal complaint is lodged or restitution is made to the company.

4. What is the best way to curtail sexual harassment in a plant or office?

   Sexual harassment may be curtailed through good educational programs and a policy that dictates that persons violating such a policy will be dealt with harshly. The company must be willing to deal with this sop that any incident will be handled expeditiously and efficiently.

5. What is your understanding of the word *predication* as it applies to private security?

   Predication is the total set of circumstances that would lead a reasonable, prudent and professionally trained person to believe that an offense has occurred, is occurring or will occur. It is not as strong as the probable cause required for public police officers to arrest someone, but it must be more than mere suspicion.

ANSWERS TO QUIZ 11

1.c, 2.d, 3.d, 4.b, 5.a, 6.d, 7.c, 8.d, 9.c, 10.d, 11.a, 12.b, 13.b, 14.c, 15.d, 16.d, 17.d, 18.d, 19.d, 20.a.

NOTES:

Notes, *continued*

Chapter 12

OBTAINING AND PROVIDING INFORMATION

OBJECTIVES

Upon completing this chapter, the student will know:

- What the communication process involves.
- What the average speaking speed is, and what the average listening or "word processing" speed is.
- What nonverbal communication and written nonverbal communication include.
- What the lines of communication are.
- How to take notes.
- What the characteristics of effective notes are.
- What are the two basic types of reports security officers write.
- Why reports are so important.
- The characteristics of a well-written report.

KEY TERMS

The student will also be able to define the following terms: administrative reports, calibrating, communication, conclusionary language, connotative words, denotative words, empathy, facts, feedback, grapevine, inferences, judgments, military time, nonverbal communication, operational reports, opinion, reports, 24-hour clock.

POSSIBLE RESPONSE TO THE APPLICATION

This is not an acceptable report. It is not factual or accurate because it states that Martinez was robbed when, in fact, he was burglarized. It is not objective because it uses the word "Spikes" and includes the opinion that "Most Spikes can't get any better jobs at the track." It is not concise; it includes such irrelevant statements as "right after coffee break." It lacks clarity; "While swearing profusely about getting ripped off, I..." makes it initially sound as though the reporting officer was swearing profusely. It is not correct; several errors in spelling occur: "lite-wait," "pear," "there" rather than "their," and "its" rather than "it's." It is also not always in standard English. Instances of nonstandard English include: "hisself," "cuz," "I seen," "real good," and "he seen."

POSSIBLE ANSWERS TO THE DISCUSSION QUESTIONS

1. Which basic communication skill--speaking, listening, reading, writing--do you have most difficulty with? Why?

   Answers will vary with students. There are remedial programs where students can correct most deficiencies within a short time. They should consult with their instructor.

2. How can security managers encourage upward communication from their officers?

   Practice, practice and more practice will lead to greater upward communication. It is the officers who participate in the management of the organization who should be impressed by how important their communications are. On the other hand, if managers do not act on lower level communications, the organization will fail to establish good lines of communication.

3. What are the most significant barriers to communication in security work?

   One of the most significant barriers to communications is a security officer's attitude toward the individual and toward the organization. There are others that students should elaborate on.

4. How can you improve your skills at note taking? At report writing?

   The more notes you take, the more efficient you will become. You will get a sense for what is and is not important in note taking. Experience and practice will improve your notetaking skills.

5. How do internal and external lines of communication differ? What must be taken into account in each? Is one more important than the other?

   Internal communication can usually be less formal than external communication. It is also more apt to be two-way communication, with feedback playing an important role. With internal communication, security officers must consider whether the person with whom they are communicating is above or below them in the organizational structure, how familiar the person is with the organization and the like. In external communication, security officers must usually be more concerned with image and representing their organization professionally. Both are equally important forms of communication.

ADDITIONAL INFORMATION

Some private security agencies tend to report only serious incidents. Unless private security agencies and officers have a well-defined reporting policy for all incidents, they will be unable to assess accurately to what extent the agency and its officers are involved in activity. Each form used by the private security agency should be evaluated for its consistency to its stated policies. The reporting system used should reflect the agency's needs and needs of the client being served. Every officer should strive to get as much information as possible when involved in or investigating an incident. Reports should be as simple as possible to complete. Reporting is essential to private security services for establishing a data base, for assigning personnel and physical resources and for giving management a frame of reference to determine effectiveness.

ANSWERS TO QUIZ 12

1.b, 2.a, 3.a, 4.c, 5.d, 6.b, 7.c, 8.b, 9.d, 10.a, 11.a, 12.a, 13.d, 14.c, 15.d, 16.d, 17.a, 18.d, 19.a, 20.b.

NOTES:

Notes, *continued*

Chapter 13

TESTIFYING IN COURT

OBJECTIVES

Upon completing this chapter, the student will know:

- What is important in testifying in court.
- What the usual sequence in a criminal trial is.
- What direct examination and cross-examination are.
- What kinds of statements are inadmissible in court.
- How to testify most effectively.
- When to use notes while testifying.
- What nonverbal elements can influence courtroom testimony positively and negatively.
- What strategies can make testifying in court more effective.
- What defense attorney tactics to anticipate.

KEY TERMS

The student will also be able to define the following terms: cross-examination, direct examination, impeaching.

POSSIBLE RESPONSE TO THE APPLICATION

You can wear all the warm and fuzzy colors and all the right power clothes and it still won't make any difference if you have a lousy case.

First of all, there is an old adage about clothes making the man. The dress of a security officer is an extremely powerful tool because it is subconscious, often connected to public law enforcement. In court, words can fool you, but clothing and body language don't fool anyone. Dressing appropriately for court helps create perceptions and expectations. Within the first 60 seconds of seeing someone testifying in the court for the first time, the person makes key impressions, among them: economic and educational status, moral character, level of sophistication and integrity. And like it or not, most of those impressions come from

50 Chapter 13

appearance. The private security officer who does not look credible may not be perceived as credible. Ninety-three percent of the impact a security officer has upon court room personnel and the jury is nonverbal.

Certain rules of thumb apply. A dark suit, for example, has "I'm worth listening to" written all over it. Traditional apparel sends the message that the wearer is trustworthy and logical. You shouldn't try to be someone you're not. If jurors pick up on one thing it's phoniness. One of the most important things about clothing is how you feel in it. In terms of clothing, that often says more to a jury than anything else.

Image is a big factor in testifying in court. Besides gaining tips on clothing and other aspects of testifying from their superiors, officers should contact the attorney whose side they will be testifying for and discuss the information the attorney will be seeking from them.

Officers should know if the attorney wants them to wear their uniforms in court. Also, they should get their notes in order and review their reports pertinent to the case. They should be warned also that any of their testimony will be attacked for its credibility, veracity and, in some cases, admissibility.

[SOURCE: Rick Nelson. "Law and Disorder: The Court Appeal." *Corporate Report of Minnesota,* January 1995, p.31.]

POSSIBLE ANSWERS TO THE DISCUSSION QUESTIONS

1. What is one of the most important documents a security officer can bring to court?

    Notes of the incident or investigation are very important. Notes are a permanent aid to an officer's memory. Good notes aid in investigating a case, in writing a report and in testifying in court. Good notes have many of the same characteristics as a good report. Good notes are clear, complete, concise, accurate and objective. Good notes are a prerequisite for a good report. Additionally, good notes enhance the case, impress jurors and lawyers and help the officer bring forth facts necessary to the case.

2. What does an attorney look for from the security officer when the officer testifies?

    Attorneys, whether a prosecutor, defense attorney or a civil litigant or civil defense lawyer, look to see that officers search for and report the truth--facts that can be verified through one of the officer's five senses: sight, hearing, touch, taste or smell. To be useful, facts must be accurate. When testifying, officers may form a conclusion or make an inference, but it must be reasoning substantiated by some type of fact.

3. Why is there so much emphasis on keeping good notes?

    The emphasis on keeping good notes is because the best way to approach accurate report writing and testimony in court is to start with good note taking. Field notes are separate from report writing, but they are exceedingly valuable in that they are usually the foundation for the actual report, which may be used in court. The private security officer who takes effective notes will find that testifying in court becomes much easier and accuracy of testimony is increased.

4. How should a security officer on the witness stand deal with an attorney who is trying to confuse him or her with rapid-fire questioning so that the answers the officer gives might be inconsistent?

    The most polite way to counter this type of tactic is for officers to take their time answering the questions. Another way to slow down an attorney's questioning is for the officer to ask to have the question repeated, thwarting the efforts at rapid-fire questioning.

5. How do most attorneys attempt to attack security officers' credibility before the jury?

    Most attorneys try to undermine an officer's credibility by focusing on any assumptions or inferences made by an officer during testimony. Assumptions and inferences are natural. We spend our whole life making assumptions. The law recognizes the validity of assumptions and inferences. As long as they are reasonable and are based on facts, courts and the jury will recognize them as being reasonable.

ANSWERS TO QUIZ 13

1.b, 2.c, 3.d, 4.d, 5.a, 6.c, 7.b, 8.d, 9.d, 10.c, 11.b, 12.d, 13.d, 14.d, 15.a, 16.a, 17.c, 18.b, 19.a, 20.c.

NOTES:

Notes, *continued*

Chapter 14

LOSS PREVENTION THROUGH RISK MANAGEMENT

OBJECTIVES

Upon completing this chapter, the student will know:

- The difference between pure and dynamic risk.
- What risk management is.
- What is included in a systematic approach to preventing loss through risk management.
- Whether risk management is a moral or a legal responsibility.
- What three factors are considered in risk analysis.
- What a security survey is.
- How the information needed for a security survey is obtained.
- What alternatives exist for handling risks.
- When components of the security system should be evaluated.

KEY TERMS

The student will also be able to define the following terms: criticality, dynamic risk, probability, pure risk, risk, risk acceptance, risk elimination, risk management, risk reduction, risk spreading, risk transfer, security survey, vulnerability.

POSSIBLE RESPONSES TO THE APPLICATION

1. The risks one is exposed to depend a great deal on the person's lifestyle and values. A simple pure risk people expose themselves to is leaving their keys in their parked automobile in a high-crime area. There is a potential for incurring a loss with no accompanying benefit. To reduce such loss, most people have automobile insurance. Dynamic risks may include investing in the stock market, participating in sports or even driving a car.

2. The list of the local hotel's security manager should include any pure and dynamic risks that might interrupt or affect the orderly flow of business such as fires, natural disasters, injury

to persons and crimes committed on the premises such as theft, prostitution or armed robbery.

Priorities should include the utmost protection of the guests, such as protection from bodily harm through fires, assaults or robberies, in that order. The likelihood of a natural disaster striking may be remotes. Prostitution is generally not a problem at most hotels, therefore low on the priority list. Room burglaries are extremely rare also and so would be low on the priority list.

3. Answers will vary depending on your state laws. You might assign some students to research these laws and report to the rest of the class.

POSSIBLE ANSWERS TO THE DISCUSSION QUESTIONS

1. What types of programs would you implement to eliminate pure risks in a company?

   To eliminate pure risks in a company, crime prevention and safety programs should be adopted in the interest of both management and the consumer. See Figure 14-1 to identify areas that should be considered.

2. How much responsibility and authority should be placed at the security supervisory level to cope with dynamic risks?

   To be effective, supervisors who are delegated responsibility must also be given the authority to act in any risk situation. Training and policy guidelines should be established to obtain the greatest possible security.

3. What could cause the needs and objectives of a security system to change? Elaborate.

   The needs and objectives of a security system can change for a variety of reasons. As society changes, so do security needs. Rising costs, mergers, new management, government regulations, state statutes and expansion plans--all could affect an established security system.

4. In developing a security survey, what areas should receive high priority?

   In developing a security survey, the areas that should received high priority are those that make a company vulnerable to a variety of risks, including both internal and external threats. Each business and industry has its vulnerable and critical areas that must be given high priority.

5. Is it better for security managers to develop their own security survey or to use one developed by someone else?

It is usually best to *adapt* an existing security system that has been used successfully. In most cases, such an adaptation will reduce the likelihood that critical vulnerable areas will be overlooked in the survey while simultaneously assuring that the survey meets the unique security needs of the establishment.

ANSWERS TO QUIZ 14

1.c, 2.d, 3.d, 4.d, 5.b, 6.b, 7.d, 8.a, 9.c, 10.d, 11.a, 12.b, 13.c, 14.c, 15.a, 16.a, 17.d, 18.c, 19.d, 20.b.

NOTES:

Notes, *continued*

Chapter 15

INDUSTRIAL SECURITY

OBJECTIVES

Upon completing this chapter, the student will know:

- What types of losses are usually specific to industry.
- How to protect against loss of tools.
- What special problems must be considered in industrial security.
- What sabotage and espionage are.
- How to protect against industrial espionage.
- What areas are most vulnerable to theft.
- What cargoes are most frequently stolen from trucks.
- What security measures have been used by the trucking industry.
- What the primary security problems of the railroad industry are.
- What security measures have been taken by railroads.
- What security problems exist at utility companies.
- How to protect against a utility company's losses.

KEY TERMS

The student will also be able to define the following terms: espionage, sabotage.

POSSIBLE RESPONSE TO THE APPLICATION

A security director who is informed that an employee was engaging in the theft of company trade secrets should undertake observation through foot, motor and photographic surveillance. Foot and motor surveillances might show the employee transferring sensitive documents to a spy or competitor. Before such an operation can be implemented, however, it is imperative that the security director consult with company executives because of the sensitivity of such an investigation and the possibility of civil liability. It may be that the magnitude of the losses incurred may not affect the company's status whatsoever. Nonetheless, it is important that the sensitive documents be recovered if possible. Planting electronic devices in strategic places and using monitoring telephone devices is discouraged because of federal restrictions on such devices and because of the Privacy Act.

If the charges were well founded and sufficient evidence warranted a criminal charge, top management and the legal staff should be consulted. A precedent may be established by going ahead with the prosecution. Also, the prosecuting attorney should be consulted as to the liability of the company should a prosecution not be successful. Resources of state and federal agencies are available in such cases and should be consulted as to what the proper procedures should be.

POSSIBLE ANSWERS TO THE DISCUSSION QUESTIONS

1. What are some preventive measures a security director might apply to guard against espionage in a computer manufacturing company?

   Preventative measures to guard against espionage in a computer manufacturing company include careful selection and screening of employees. Tight security in vulnerable plant areas can be a deterrent. Handling of classified materials such as logs and documents should be restricted to only authorized personnel.

2. Name several effective ways to protect vital documents and records from destruction or theft.

   Important, irreplaceable data should be safeguarded in fireproof safes or vaults. The rooms containing these safes and vaults should have adequate protective devices, including strong locks, and access control should be assured. The security director must tailor the security safeguards based on the type of documents to be protected.

3. What methods might espionage agents use to undermine a competitor?

   A variety of methods of espionage have been used to undermine competitors, including unscheduled strikes, work slowdowns, deliberate alterations of product standards and encouragement of employees to cause production breakdowns by deliberately misusing equipment and raw materials. Competitors might also steal vital documents, including long-range plans, new products under development and marketing strategies. They might also hire away key employees.

4. What are some reasons employees engage in sabotage?

   Employees engage in sabotage for several reasons. Some employees have personal problems that escalate, or they may have an exaggerated grievance against the employer.

Persons in this state of mind have no fear of punishment; the acts committed are justifiable under the circumstances in their own minds.

5. What security measures are effective in minimizing the possibility of cargo theft from trucks? Railroad cars?

   Security measures to minimize cargo theft from truck and railroad cars include visual observation, surveillances, CCTV and alarm systems. Metal seal bars are also often used.

ADDITIONAL INFORMATION

Industrial espionage carried out by employee spies is common in today's competitive business world. It is not uncommon for competing business people to shop each other's marketing products to compare prices, quality and selling techniques. This is legal, however, and part of today's business world. It is the employee who steals from the company we are concerned about. The employee who is either unfaithful, highly in debt, blackmailed or who otherwise compromises his principles is detrimental to the company's operation.

Sometimes even top company executives inadvertently fall prey to industrial spying by revealing classified data under the guise of expressing good will or while in conversation with strangers at bars. Industrial spies are difficult to detect. They can be company research scientists, chemists, managers, production employees, secretaries or custodians. A security manager must be ever alert for signs of industrial espionage.

ANSWERS TO QUIZ 15

1.d, 2.a, 3.d, 4.a, 5.b, 6.c, 7.a, 8.c, 9.d, 10.d, 11.b, 12.b, 13.d, 14.c, 15.d, 16.b, 17.a, 18.b, 19.d, 20.b.

NOTES:

Notes, *continued*

Chapter 16

RETAIL SECURITY

OBJECTIVES

Upon completing this chapter, the student will know:

- What crimes are most frequently committed against retail establishments.
- What legally constitutes shoplifting.
- How shoplifters are classified.
- What methods are commonly used to shoplift.
- What preventive measures can be taken to curtail shoplifting.
- What basic difference exists between security officers and floorwalkers.
- What merchandising techniques, procedures and physical controls can be used to deter shoplifting.
- When and how to apprehend individuals suspected of shoplifting.
- What factors influence when prosecution is advisable.
- How to deter losses from bad checks.
- Which types of checks are considered high-risk checks.
- What the most common types of bad checks are.
- How checks should be examined.
- What identification to require.
- How to deter losses from credit cards.
- What types of employee theft frequently occur in retail establishments and what preventive measures can be taken.
- What honesty shopping is.
- What the two primary objectives of shopping center security are.

KEY TERMS

The student will also be able to define the following terms: booster box, floor release limit, floorwalkers, honesty shopping, kleptomaniac, prima facie evidence, probable cause, reasonable cause, shoplifting, shopping service, sliding, zero floor release limit.

POSSIBLE RESPONSES TO THE APPLICATION

1. Officer Benson should determine in private what the manager of the liquor store wants to do. If he wants to press charges, then Officer Benson should question the suspect about the charges the manager has made. At this point, depending on what the suspect says, Officer Benson may arrest him for theft. Whether he reads the suspect the Miranda warning depends on the store's policy. It is *not* legally required in most states.

2. The security director should recommend that the management try to settle out of court. Although police officers have the right to break a window of a vehicle to arrest a suspect, private security officers do not have such a right.

3. The retail security checklist is very complete. Of course, such checklists will vary from one establishment to another depending on what is sold and what type of building is used.

4. Nothing needs to be added to the form. Regardless of how legal a form appears, it must not contain any words that would be construed to make promises to the employee for confessing, or to intimidate the employee, or to in any way mislead the employee as to the ramifications of signing such a form. All releases should be evaluated and approved by the company's legal counsel so that, should a lawsuit emanate as a result of a dismissal, general counsel would be aware of what the form contained and could properly establish a defense for the security personnel's actions.

POSSIBLE ANSWERS TO THE DISCUSSION QUESTIONS

1. What are the advantages and disadvantages of prosecuting juvenile shoplifters? Adult shoplifters?

    One perceived advantage of prosecuting shoplifters, be they juvenile or adults, is that they will be out of circulation for some time. From a sociological and psychological standpoint, it is beneficial to prosecute both juvenile and adult shoplifters because soon the word will get around regarding the store's tough policy concerning shoplifting. On the other hand, prosecuting juveniles or adults for minor shoplifting incidents may cost the store too much money in time and manpower to make it worthwhile. Discretion must be used in these cases.

2. What type of system would aid retail stores in combating bad-check artists?

   When a substantial bad check, such as a counterfeit payroll check, has been cashed and it is discovered shortly after the transaction, an umbrella-type telephoning system alerting each store frequently stifles the passer. One store alerts two stores who in turn alert two stores each, continuing in this manner until all stores in the network have been notified. This system has worked well in cities under 100,000 population.

3. How can retail stores aid one another in preventing shoplifting? What is done in your area?

   Retail stores can aid each other in preventing shoplifting in several ways. The exchange of information, MOs and pictures when available all aid in alerting various stores as to what shoplifters are operating and what specific merchandise they are trying to steal. Monthly meetings of retail security managers and personnel are also valuable in aiding each other through the exchange of information.

4. What considerations should be evaluated when a private security officer notices that an employee is stealing?

   The first consideration to evaluate when a private security officer notices that an employee is stealing is whether proof of the stealing is available. Once this is obtained, the matter should be brought to the director of personnel and the employee usually should be fired. The security officer should also determine what factors allowed for stealing to occur and whether such factors could be changed to prevent future thefts.

5. What training devices might be used in conducting a shoplifting reduction seminar?

   Training devices that might be used in conducting a shoplifting reduction seminar include films, other visual aids and demonstrations of shoplifting techniques. In addition, most local police departments have at their disposal shoplifting paraphernalia that could be exhibited to employees so they might be aware of what to look for.

ADDITIONAL INFORMATION

A silent revolution has been occurring within retail security from the old line of stereotyped operations to a modern concept of professional personnel and sophisticated technology. The increasing losses during the past decade with various impacts on narrowing profit margins have given the idea of loss prevention new value and importance. To maximize the efforts to reduce losses in retail operations, the security manager must remember that people not only cause losses, they can also prevent them. Shoplifters can be controlled, and internal theft can be prevented, as can errors in paperwork.

ANSWERS TO QUIZ 16

1.c, 2.d, 3.c, 4.a, 5.d, 6.c, 7.b, 8.b, 9.a, 10.c, 11.a, 12.b, 13.a, 14.b, 15.d, 16.d, 17.a, 18.b, 19.d, 20.a.

NOTES:

Chapter 17

COMMERCIAL SECURITY

OBJECTIVES

Upon completing this chapter, the student will know:

- What commercial enterprises rely heavily on private security.
- What specific security problems are encountered in each type of enterprise.
- What targets are most common in each.
- What special security precautions are implemented to protect the assets of each.
- What is required by the Bank Protection Act.
- What agency regulates security of airports and airlines.

KEY TERMS

The student will also be able to define the following terms: backstretch area, bait money, core concept, Dram Shop Acts, skips.

POSSIBLE RESPONSES TO THE APPLICATION

1. Answers will vary depending on the facilities selected.
2. The Mecklenberg County Police Burglary Prevention materials are educationally sound. The use of visuals helps assure that all vulnerable areas are checked. In addition to the visuals, the checklist provides a double check on the key security risk areas.

POSSIBLE ANSWERS TO THE DISCUSSION QUESTIONS

1. Why is a properly trained security staff an asset to the hotel/motel business?

    A properly trained security staff is an asset to the hotel/motel business because this industry faces an ever-increasing problem of theft by both employees and guests. The prevalence of criminal damage to property, trespassing incidents, robberies, deceptive practices, burglaries and narcotics traffic require the services of a properly trained staff. Hotel/motel security staffs are confronted with many potentially explosive situations such as a guest who decides to seek the companionship of a prostitute and becomes instead a robbery victim. A thief may obtain a master key and systematically go through guests' rooms, relieving them of their valuables. A guest who shows visible signs of wealth such as jewelry or a large roll of money may be vulnerable to mugging or burglary. Loiterers, transients and dishonest guests pose different problems for the security staff to deal with. It is the security staff's responsibility to reduce the hazards and promote prevention-oriented hotel/motel security.

2. What are some legal requirements of hotels/motels that guests of the establishment should know?

A hotel/motel is usually legally required to inform guests of any circumstances that might affect their safety, for example exposure to crime, fire or any other hazard. Maps of egress and ingress should be posted, and guests should be informed of the rules covering valuables and where they may be kept. Local and state laws regarding such things as registration and the guests' responsibilities should also be clearly posted.

3. What areas of security does the Bank Protection Act ignore?

The Bank Protection Act does not cover crimes that originate within the bank such as theft, fraud and embezzlement, even though these constitute the major loss areas for banks. Perhaps it was thought that such crimes could be covered adequately by the surprise examinations of the Federal Deposit Insurance Corporation (FDIC), state banking examiners or the bank's internal auditor.

4. Which types of security discussed in this chapter seems most important to you? Why?

Answers will vary.

5. Which public gatherings in your area might pose a security problem?

Again, answers will vary. Crowd control at public gatherings is considered dangerous and is a major problem for both public and private police. The heightening of emotions, whether at a convention, rock concert or sporting event, endangers the safety of the officers in charge. Good planning by the security director may alleviate many problems that could otherwise lead to confrontations. Security directors charged with crowd control at major events must plan, direct, organize and coordinate all efforts to assure that the peace is maintained.

SUGGESTED ACTIVITIES

1. Have students visit a local financial institution and interview a security officer regarding the Bank Protection Act and observe how they have put it into effect.

2. Have students visit a commercial security enterprise that has a proprietary security force. Interview the manager and note the responsibilities of the private security officers on the premises.

ANSWERS TO QUIZ 17

1.a, 2.b, 3.d, 4.c, 5.d, 6.c, 7.c, 8.a, 9.a, 10.c, 11.d, 12.a, 13.d, 14.a, 15.a, 16.b, 17.c, 18.c, 19.a, 20.c.

NOTES:

Notes, *continued*

Chapter 18

INSTITUTIONAL SECURITY

OBJECTIVES

Upon completing this chapter, the student will know:

- What institutions may require special security.
- What security problems exist at health care facilities.
- What security problems exist at educational facilities.
- What security problems exist at libraries.
- What security problems exist at museums and art galleries.
- What security problems exist at religious facilities.
- What security measures can be taken to avoid or reduce these problems.

KEY TERMS

The student will also be able to define the following terms: ARTCENTRAL, ethnoviolence, INTERPOL, photogrammetry.

POSSIBLE RESPONSES TO THE APPLICATIONS

1. These checklists will vary with each individual. Each facility discussed in this chapter is unique; no standardized checklist would cover all needs in these facilities. Each requires a different approach and a different protection plan. Students should discuss the various needs of each facility and how they are reflected in their checklists.

2. These educational materials *are* effective for institutional security.

POSSIBLE ANSWERS TO THE DISCUSSION QUESTIONS

1. Which types of security discussed in this chapter seem most important to you? Why?

   Answers will vary considerably as to what types of security seem most important.

2. How can security directors enhance the public relations of a health care facility?

   Security directors can enhance the public relations of a health care facility in many ways. High visibility through foot and motor patrols throughout the hospital and grounds often helps develop a psychological sense of well being. Access control, either in the hospital itself or to various parts of the hospital premises, is another area requiring good public relations. It, too, develops a sense of security and well being.

3. What kind of security is provided at your campus?

   Campus security problems are universal. Crimes against property and persons occur daily. Vandalizing of equipment and buildings is a major threat. With student demonstrations and unrest on many campuses, emotional outbursts often lead to attacks on security officers. Burglaries, thefts, rapes and assaults are the most prevalent crimes against which security officers must establish prevention programs. The types of security systems used on various campuses will vary considerably, as will the problems associated with these systems.

4. Do you have art galleries or museums in your community that might be at risk? If so, what kind of security do they have?

   Not every community has galleries or museums; however, if there are some in the student's community, it may be educational to visit and see what type of security is afforded the valuable items.

5. Have there been instances of crimes committed against any religious facilities in your community?

   There may not have been sufficient publicity to bring this type of crime to the attention of the general public.

ADDITIONAL INFORMATION

Every health care facility must have good security as it may mean the difference of operating in the black or operating at a deficit. The question most frequently asked in establishing a health care security system is what type of security is necessary--patrols, fire and safety, security against vandalism, internal theft or security of assets. Should the health care facility hire its own personnel or should it contract the services to cover the institution? To make such decisions, security directors must consider the size of the facility, its location, the number of employees, the number of visitors and the specific security problems involved.

Surveillance of the pharmacy area is critical in all health care facilities. Using a unit-dose system (progressive inventory) throughout the facility will greatly reduce drug loss. The narcotics safe or room should be wired to an alarm that rings loudly when unauthorized persons try to enter. In any health care facility, security officers should be equipped with walkie-talkie radios so they can contact each other within seconds.

ANSWERS TO QUIZ 18

1.c, 2.b, 3.a, 4.d, 5.d, 6.a, 7.d, 8.b, 9.d, 10.b, 11.b, 12.b, 13.d, 14.a, 15.b, 16.d, 17.b, 18.a, 19.a, 20.d.

NOTES:

Notes, *continued*

Chapter 19

OTHER APPLICATIONS OF SECURITY AT WORK

OBJECTIVES

Upon completing this chapter, the student will know:

- In what other areas security systems are frequently in place.
- What security problems exist in parking lots and ramps and how these problems might be reduced.
- What security problems exist in the courtroom and how such problems might be reduced.
- What security problems exist in protecting VIPs, corporate executives and political candidates and how these problems might be reduced.
- What problems exist in businesses located abroad and how such problems might be reduced.

KEY TERMS

The student will also be able to define the following terms: choke points, preincident indicators.

POSSIBLE RESPONSES TO THE APPLICATIONS

You are in luck. Your supervisor not only is considered an expert in parking lot management but also teaches a course at the community college which awards continuing education credits upon completion of the course.

A parking lot manager would tell you that his job brings him nothing but complaints and headaches. But all parking lot managers will tell you that the focus is on service to the customer, whether it is a visitor, a customer, an employee or a vendor, and that there is a responsibility to protect the rights of these individuals.

The service given also takes the form of direct communications with all the people who use the facility. Therefore, when the services that you perform were delivered, it also enhanced your image, your employer's image and the company that hired you. You are also obligated to protect the rights of individuals who have been assigned certain areas to park, such as the handicapped or employees who are designated preferential parking because of their status in the company. Also, the security officer must be aware of temporary permits which may be issued to students who are temporarily employed or to construction workers. The driving force in the nineties has been quality service. Developing a parking program is one way to improve not only your department's or company's visibility, but to emphasize your service orientation and overall security program.

POSSIBLE ANSWERS TO THE DISCUSSION QUESTIONS

1. In your experience with parking lots and ramps, do you find that most have taken some measures to provide security?

   In today's society, almost all parking lots and ramps have some type of security. In some cases, security officers are present, making their checks and their rounds to provide a degree of safety. Some ramps and lots are flooded with lighting that aids in crime prevention. There are also closed circuit television monitors (CCTV) which are monitored by security officers. Some ramps have 24-hour service with individuals on the premises not only to provide safety but to collect the parking fees. Other sophisticated pieces of equipment are also available.

2. What are some security problems American businesspeople confront when in a foreign country?

   In a worldwide economy, western business executives frequently become the targets for terrorists. It is because of the rapid growth of the democratic countries and their emphasis on personal wealth rather than religion that in many cases brings to them the label of the devil. Therefore, they are frequent targets for assassination. Those in the diplomatic corps stationed in foreign countries are also the target of those who wish to drive them out of certain countries, fearing their influence on the population there. Keeping a low profile is one problem these diplomatic employees have.

3. Review the Critical Thinking Application regarding the University of Nebraska case. Mahlberg was a proprietary security officer, hired by and working for the University of Nebraska. Do you think that if the University had used a private security agency for its security personnel this would have happened?

   The odds of it happening with a contractual agency would be less likely than with the proprietary type of security the University of Nebraska had. A contractual agency would have had enough personnel to rotate them consistently so they would not be so familiar with the beat Mahlberg had. On the other hand, it is very difficult to predict human behavior.

4. In the case of the terrorist assassination of German businessman Alfred Herrhausen, what would have been Herrhausen's best protection according to the experts?

As pointed out by Scotti, "surveillance detection" would have been of benefit and may have saved Herrhausen's life. He emphasizes "choke points" that should be checked out because this is where ambush is most likely to occur. Here, advance observations made by individuals responsible for "surveillance detection" can do a lot to protect lives and property.

5. Why do people feel uneasy about walking late at night through parking garages or ramps?

Usually because they instill fear. If they are not well lit, they may bring terror into the hearts of many. The emphasis in movies, on television and in crime prevention programs has visualized the parking garage or ramp as a place where crime has run rampant. We have seen scenes in the movies and on television showing car chases through parking ramps and garages, gun battles, stabbings and women getting assaulted. No wonder we fear entering a parking garage or ramp at night. No one ever advertises how safe their ramps are or that the ramp or garage is monitored by surveillance equipment 24 hours a day.

ANSWERS TO QUIZ 19

1.a, 2.d, 3.d, 4.b, 5.c, 6.a, 7.d, 8.c, 9.d, 10.d, 11.a, 12.d, 13.b, 14.b, 15.c, 16.c, 17.c, 18.d, 19.a, 20.b.

NOTES:

Notes, *continued*

Chapter 20

THE CHALLENGES OF VIOLENCE IN THE WORKPLACE

OBJECTIVES

Upon completing this chapter, the student will know:

- How extensive workplace violence is.
- What forms violence in the workplace may take.
- What are potential causes of such violence.
- What are characteristics of the typical perpetrator of workplace violence.
- What might be predictors of workplace violence.
- What factors might increase a worker's risk of being a victim of violence.
- What steps might be taken to prevent workplace violence.
- What should be done if workplace violence occurs.

KEY TERM

The student will also be able to define the following term: toxic work environment.

POSSIBLE RESPONSES TO THE APPLICATIONS

1. The problem the security officer has with confronting Keith Wilson is that the officer does not know what is on his mind. Confronting him might lead to extreme violence, and the security officer has not had time to formulate a plan. This alternative has certain risks to it and should be evaluated with some other alternatives.

2. For a security officer to call the public police before conferring with others in authority again might expose employees or others to risks that could be minimized by considering other alternatives. Put this one on hold unless instructed by higher authority to call the public police.

3. Not a bad idea, except no action means some action is going to be forthcoming and that might be violence. Temporarily, this is a good idea, but an assessment of a course of action must be made.

4. A very good idea. What is your security company policy about making a move to resolve this type of tense situation? Maybe there could be too much liability for your company to take any steps before another assessment. Your supervisor will probably say that alternative number five is the way to go.

5. Notify company management. This is the proper thing to do. After all, you have been hired by this company, and they should be the ones to be notified. They also should be the ones to make the decision as to what course of action they might prefer or take. This way, you have done your utmost, prevented any violence from occurring and taken a proper course of action. From here on, it is management's responsibility to deal with the situation.

POSSIBLE ANSWERS TO THE DISCUSSION QUESTIONS

1. Statistics released by the U.S. Department of Justice on violence in the workplace indicate that more than half of all workplace victimizations were never reported to the police. Discuss why this occurs.

   A variety of reasons have been given by various individuals as to why workplace violence has not been reported to the public police. More than half stated that they had not reported it to the police. Forty percent believed that the incident was too minor to report or decided to keep it as a private matter. An additional 27 percent did not report their victimization to the police because they stated they had reported it to the company security guard. Even though some incidents had been reported to the police, the company in most cases did not report it, fearing adverse media publicity. They handled it internally.

2. Do you think that security officers working in highly emotionally charged areas should undertake preventive measures in the interest of employee safety? What should their role be?

   This depends on the policy of the security department, or in the case of a contractual agency, what their policy might be. If individuals are going to be responsible for preventive measures and intervention, they must be highly trained. Most companies today do not want to spend the money for training in this area.

3. Recently a University of Iowa doctoral student who had lost a cherished dissertation prize stated just before killing five people that the gun was a "great equalizer." What comments do you have about a person who takes such forceful measures to show his feelings?

   Unfortunately, the gun is what the student had stated as a "great equalizer." Firearms play a key role in violence in the workplace. Not only does the gun correct the power imbalance between employees and their superiors, but it is simply far more lethal, particularly when the employee wants to pursue multiple victims. The gun also has a tendency to psychologically distance the attacker from his victims. Although the person might be full of rage, they might be deterred were it necessary to kill with their hands. A gun makes killing very easy.

4. Is it possible to screen prospective employees for violence proneness?

   It might not be feasible or even possible for various reasons of privacy to assemble as complete an investigation to weed out undesirable recruits. For instance, the Americans with Disabilities Act of 1990 may restrict screening on the basis of clinical depression, unless it is clear that the job recruit is prone to become violent. There are clues, however, that you can recognize, such as a person constantly being tense, belligerent, paranoid or appearing to despise authority.

5. Whose responsibility do you think it is to see that violence prevention policies are established?

   Company management is responsible for establishing violence prevention policies. Unfortunately, many businesses do not invest as much time and effort in firing as they do in hiring. Rather than take a proactive approach in the procedures for termination and layoffs, they ignore the potential for employee violence unless, of course, a threat has been made.

ANSWERS TO QUIZ 20

1.c, 2.d, 3.b, 4.d, 5.d, 6.a, 7.d, 8.a, 9.d, 10.c, 11.d, 12.b, 13.d, 14.a, 15.d, 16.c, 17.d, 18.a, 19.d, 20.d.

NOTES:

Notes, *continued*

Chapter 21

PRACTICING AND PROMOTING ETHICAL CONDUCT

OBJECTIVES

Upon completing this chapter, the student will know:

- What the term "ethics" refers to.
- What three personal ethics-check questions are.
- What five principles underlie individual ethical power.
- What three organizational ethics-check questions are.
- What purpose is served by a code of ethics for security professionals.
- How to promote an ethical organization.
- How ethics can relate to problem solving.

KEY TERMS

The student will also be able to define the following terms: code of ethics, ethical behavior, ethics, moral.

POSSIBLE RESPONSES TO THE APPLICATION

It is unfortunate that Johnny Abrams, as a person being paid to supervise and advise subordinates, does not offer Officer Hynes suggestions as to what he should do. The fact that Officer Hynes let George Simon off with a verbal warning may indicate two things: (1) the officer had no experience in handling this type of situation and (2) did not realize that sending him back to his job under the influence of a drug may have been devastating to other employees, particularly if Simon was working with highly volatile chemicals, machinery or any type of work that could lead to a disaster.

It may have been a fair decision in Officer Hynes' mind, but it seems he took the easy way out. It definitely was not a good decision from any aspect--the security officer, his supervisor, George Simon, his supervisor and the company.

The actions of Johnny Abrams, the supervisor and Elmer Hynes undoubtedly perpetuated the use of cocaine by George Simon. Had the private security officers notified George's immediate supervisor at the time of the incident, he could have been placed into a company-sponsored drug rehabilitation program. This would have been the correct action to take in this situation.

POSSIBLE ANSWERS TO THE DISCUSSION QUESTIONS

1. Security personnel, whether guards, supervisors or managers, frequently are in a position to obtain information that could prove embarrassing to a company that relies on the contractual or the proprietary services to see that the business is creating a good image and that all violations of unethical conduct are handled in a manner conducive to good company business. To uphold this philosophy, as a security supervisor or manager, how would you proceed?

   Much will depend on the size of the force, the chain of command and company policy. In smaller organizations it may be that each individual, without much guidance, would have to use their own discretion as to reporting procedures. In a larger security organization, written policies and procedures would give the security officers guidance and make unethical matters more manageable as they would be handled only by upper management of the security force. Certainly it is neither productive nor rewarding for anyone in an organization to "go along to get along" with less ethical employees. Companies must face these ethical challenges through education, training and a desire to enforce whatever is necessary.

2. Which is more serious--unethical behavior by a business or unethical behavior by the contractual agency that the business hired?

   Neither one is acceptable; however, any unethical behavior by a security agency certainly taints the whole industry. The security agency represents honesty, integrity, truthfulness and principles. It must abide by its ethical code and be an example for all of what private security agencies represent. As sometimes happens, the contractual agency comes upon an employer who is unethical in their business dealings and asks the contractual agency to participate in its transactions. The honest, reliable and outstanding agency should not participate with such an employer. In the long run, it will affect their own ability to contract with other companies.

3. Johnny McGuire, a security officer at the Glenview Nursing Home, during the hours of midnight to 8:00 a.m., makes coffee during the course of his shift without the knowledge of the complex managers and periodically has a cup to stay awake. What is your opinion of this unsupervised activity?

   This may seem like a bit of a minor violation to deal with, but eventually this type of activity could very well get Johnny McGuire and his security company in serious trouble. It is always an ethical question as to whether one should acquire the goods of another, even though it may be minor, without just compensation. In this decade of tight fiscal management, it may be that the management would prefer McGuire bring his own coffee or refrain altogether from this shift activity. However, he could avoid an otherwise embarrassing situation by getting permission from the manager of the nursing home.

4. Do you believe ethics are only for those who are vulnerable?

   Ethics is for everyone. A Code of Ethics promotes an awareness by employers and employees of their obligations to their effective performance and sense of pride. The guides for conduct provided in the code of ethics also allow private security personnel to carry out their duties with discretion and professionalism. We may falsely assume that just because *we* are ethics conscious, everyone else is. Many people in the working field have never heard of ethics. These people must be reached and educated.

5. What are the additional benefits of adopting and enforcing a code of ethics?

   By promoting a climate of professionalism in which one can experience personal satisfaction and worth, the code of ethics can help companies and agencies retain efficient, capable personnel and attract new security officers of a higher caliber. It sets forth professional guidelines for everyone so that everyone operates on a level playing field. It is a step toward increased professionalism and status.

ANSWERS TO QUIZ 21

1.d, 2.c, 3.b, 4.a, 5.d, 6.d, 7.b, 8.c, 9.a, 10.d, 11.d, 12.d, 13.a, 14.b, 15.d, 16.d, 17.c, 18.c, 19.a, 20.d.

NOTES:

Notes, *continued*

Chapter 22

THE PRIVATE SECURITY PROFESSIONAL AND PROFESSION

OBJECTIVES

Upon completing this chapter, the student will know:

- Where in an establishment's organizational structure private security fits.
- What roles a security director fills.
- What administrative, investigative and managerial responsibilities a security director has.
- What the primary goal of a private security system is.
- What a SMART objective is.
- How employees and management can be educated about the security/safety system.
- What the basic investigative skills are.
- What areas security directors are responsible for investigating.
- What the managerial responsibilities of security directors are.
- What preemployment qualifications should be met by private security personnel.
- What constitutes adequate preemployment screening.
- How effective job performance of security officers can be increased.
- When training of security officers should occur.
- What progressive discipline is.

KEY TERMS

The student will also be able to define the following terms: affirmative action, agenda, andragogy, authoritarian, authority, bureaucratic, delegation, democratic, dictatorial, discipline, Equal Employment Opportunity Commission (EEOC), firearm, goals, grievance, hierarchy, hierarchy of needs, job description, management, management by objectives (MBO), manager, mentor, morale, motivate, Occupational Safety and Health Act of 1970 (OSHAct), on-line personnel, pedagogy, performance appraisal, permissive, SMART objectives, span of management (or control), supervisor, unity of command.

POSSIBLE RESPONSES TO THE APPLICATION

1. The serious consequences for both employers and employees in private security when untrained persons are assigned to responsibilities that require firearms are obvious. There is always the possibility of self-injury due to mishandling of the weapon. Injury to innocent bystanders may occur because of the lack of skill when firing the weapon. As a result, criminal and civil suits may be filed against both the employee and the employer. Insurance rates are considerably higher if private security officers carry weapons. In most cases, proprietary officers can be justified in carrying weapons, particularly those who work in manufacturing plants dealing with government defense contracts. Officers working armored cars are also justified in carrying weapons. The problems exist when officers carrying weapons are not adequately trained.

2. Other than wearing a clean uniform and being well groomed and presentable, the image of the private security officer will come from the officer's personality. Security officers must have poise, self-confidence and the ability to adapt themselves to the environment in which they work. It is not a super-human image, but one of kindness and interest in people's well-being that security officers should project.

3. Job descriptions will vary from organization to organization as well as from proprietary to contractual. For this application, the class could be divided into small groups to work together devising a job description for one specific area.

POSSIBLE ANSWERS TO THE DISCUSSION QUESTIONS

1. How can private security directors enhance the image of the private security officer?

   Private security directors can enhance the image of the private security officer by providing encouragement and recognition of a job well done to increase the security officer's self-esteem. It is imperative that supervisors maintain a good interpersonal relationship with their subordinates to reach the organization's desired goals.

2. List the resources one might use to obtain qualified people to hire as security officers.

   Resources available to obtain qualified people to hire as security officers include advertisements in college papers and in city newspapers. An additional source is the recommendation of persons already working for the agency.

3. What are three characteristics of a good training program?

   Three characteristics of a good training program are qualified instructors, meaningful and useful subject matter, and effective feedback to students.

4. What are the minimum requirements for an effective security officer?

   Minimum requirements for an effective security officer include the minimum preemployment age, education and physical standards; orientation to the organization and training in all aspects of the security system of which they are a part.

5. What additional qualifications are required for a security supervisor? A security director?

   Various positions require various qualifications. Certainly supervisors and directors should have training in assets protection. It is also desirable that all security managers and supervisors be designated CPPs (Certified Protection Professionals). This program is actively being promoted by the American Society for Industrial Security and consists of evaluations and examinations in various areas of assets protection.

ADDITIONAL INFORMATION

On-going training of security personnel is an important function of security directors. Of great assistance in such training are films and slide-cassette programs.

AIMS Media (film and video) now has available a series of eight films designed for individuals or group instruction or novice or experienced personnel. The films may be purchased for $320 per film or rented for $75 per film (for five days). Cost of the entire series is $2,195.00. The films are also available on videocassette. In addition, they have a slide-cassette series that includes 12 individual programs, each 15 minutes long, that may be purchased for $55 per program. For further information on these programs, contact: AIMS Media, 6901 Woodley Avenue, Van Nuys, CA 91406 -- (818) 785-4111 or toll-free (800) 367-2467.

ANSWERS TO QUIZ 22

1.d, 2.c, 3.c, 4.a, 5.b, 6.d, 7.d, 8.a, 9.a, 10.d, 11.c, 12.d, 13.a, 14.b, 15.a, 16.c, 17.d, 18.c, 19.a, 20.b.

NOTES:

Notes, *continued*

Chapter 23

A LOOK TO THE FUTURE

OBJECTIVES

Upon completing this chapter, the student will know:

- How to view change.
- What experts say regarding the challenges ahead and what the future of the security profession holds.

KEY TERM

The student will also be able to define the following term: outsourcing.

POSSIBLE RESPONSES TO THE APPLICATION

1. Fear of crime in America is increasing. With that, the private security industry is expanding at an unprecedented rate. Today, governmental efforts are not preventing, detecting or controlling crime. The cost of economic crime is increasing, and the victims are business and industry. It is impossible to determine what the costs of uncontrolled crime waves are.

    Private security is seeking better educated applicants, both women and minorities. The rapid growth of closed-circuit television, sophisticated alarm systems, access control systems and other technology requires a more educated security specialist. Managers are needed, training must be upgraded to meet the demands and there must be industry-imposed standards. Also, accreditation programs are needed to bring the private security industry up to a professional level.

2. The future holds more moves for privatization of some public police tasks being taken over by the private security industry. Potential areas being taken over by privatization are court security, noninjury accident investigation, government and public event security, jail security and possible crime prevention activities. Some cities and states have already moved to have private security take over tasks previously performed by the public police such as parking enforcement, parking lot enforcement, nuclear test site security, airport security, prisoner transportation and some traffic control during peak hours. Some tasks and responsibilities could never be transferred to private security as they are embedded in the Constitution of the United States.

3. Within the private security industry, the growth of alarm firms and systems has been phenomenal. With nearly 13,000 alarm companies and 2,200 locksmiths, huge sales are being generated. Stimulation has come from the potential of telephone companies entering the market, the growth of over-the-counter sales and do-it-yourself systems, tax credits and insurance premium reductions, car alarms being installed as standard equipment and constantly improved alarm systems with capabilities of handling more alarm systems through alarm transmissions and radio frequency.

POSSIBLE ANSWERS TO THE DISCUSSION QUESTIONS

1. What skills and knowledge would an individual need to find opportunities in the private security field?

    The private security industry is constantly striving for professionalism and higher standards. Knowledge and skills beyond those associated with the security field are clearly needed and involve communications, critical thinking and problem solving intuitive management. Individuals who acquire those skills will find they are in demand in private security.

2. To ensure upward mobility in a private security agency, what characteristics and experience should be acquired?

    Getting some experience with a private security agency is helpful, plus a good background in the criminal justice field, such as a two- or four-year degree. Learn as much as you can about the tools of the industry: access control, CCTV cameras, security surveys, alarm systems and other areas that would give you a well-rounded educational and experience field.

3. What is your understanding of the word *outsourcing*?

    There is a very rapid growth of "outsourcing," which is the current term for contracting security services by private corporations and government agencies.

4. What dramatic changes in society will affect the nature of private security?

    Dramatic changes include a work force that is older and includes more women and flex- and part-time workers. Also, many in the future workforce will be working out of their homes.

5. The private security experts are predicting that "new players" will enter the field of private security in the future. Who are they talking about?

    There will be consolidation of security companies, with mega-corporations the size of IBM coming on the scene. This will drive the industry to a higher plateau in terms of research, spending and revenues. On the downside, many smaller companies could be driven out of business.

ANSWERS TO QUIZ 23

1.a, 2.d, 3.b, 4.c, 5.d, 6.a, 7.d, 8.d, 9.d, 10.a, 11.c, 12.b, 13.a, 14.d, 15.c, 16.d, 17.a, 18.d, 19.a, 20.b.

NOTES:

Notes, *continued*

CHAPTER QUIZZES

The quizzes that follow can be copied for classroom use. In most instances space is provided at the end of the quiz for the instructor to add additional questions. Sometimes the "Do You Know" questions at the beginning of the chapter can be cast in the form of brief essay questions.

Quiz One   Name:_____

THE EVOLUTION OF PRIVATE SECURITY: A BRIEF HISTORY

Select the one best answer for each of the following and put its letter in the blank to the left.

_____ 1. In ancient times, security people relied on (a) weapons and physical barriers (b) the tithing system (c) the Frankpledge system (d) all of the preceding.

_____ 2. In the Middle Ages, security people relied on (a) a primitive police force (b) the Frankpledge system (c) the military (d) both a and b.

_____ 3. In the Middle Ages, some merchants hired private police to (a) guard their establishments (b) investigate crimes against them (c) recover stolen property for them (d) all of the preceding.

_____ 4. The first public law enforcement agency in England was organized in the (a) sixteenth century (b) seventeenth century (c) eighteenth century (d) nineteenth century.

_____ 5. The tithing system and the Frankpledge system provided for (a) due process of law (b) funds to maintain an army (c) collective responsibility for law and order (d) all of the preceding.

_____ 6. In England, "due process" was provided by (a) Pitts Reform Bill (b) the Magna Charta (c) the Middlesex Justice Bill (d) the tithing system.

_____ 7. The Statute of Westminster established the (a) assize of arms (b) hue and cry (c) watch and ward (d) all of the preceding.

_____ 8. One of the earliest and most articulate advocates of crime prevention was (a) C. Reith (b) William Pitt (c) Henry Fielding (d) Sir Robert Peel.

_____ 9. The bill establishing the London Metropolitan Police was written by (a) Henry Fielding (b) Patrick Colquhoun (c) Sir Robert Peel (d) none of the preceding.

_____ 10. The principle objective of the London Metropolitan Police was to (a) prevent crime (b) suppress riots (c) investigate crimes (d) apprehend criminals.

_____ 11. In 1800, statistics on crime were compiled and used to support the need for a police force by (a) Sir Robert Peel (b) Patrick Colquhoun (c) William Pitt (d) Henry Fielding.

_____ 12. The primary means of security in the United States prior to the mid-1800s were (a) constables and night townwatchmen (b) public law enforcement officers (c) sheriffs and deputies (d) lord mayors and their magistrates.

_____ 13. The first law enforcement officer hired to protect the railroads was (a) Washington Perry Brink (b) Edwin Holmes (c) Allan Pinkerton (d) William J. Burns.

Quiz One, page 2

_____ 14. The first contract private security operation in the United States was established by (a) Washington Perry Brink (b) Edwin Holmes (c) Allan Pinkerton (d) William J. Burns.

_____ 15. In the early 1900s, the sole investigating agency for the American Banking Association was founded by (a) William J. Burns (b) Edwin Holmes (c) Washington Perry Brink (d) Allan Pinkerton.

_____ 16. Armored car and courier services in the United States were established by (a) William J. Burns (b) Washington Perry Brink (c) Loomis (d) Wells Fargo.

_____ 17. The railroad police (a) were unhampered by jurisdictional constraints (b) provided the sole means of law enforcement in many parts of the country for a period of time (c) were often granted general police powers (d) all of the preceding.

_____ 18. The world wars heightened emphasis on security in (a) the government (b) industrial plants (c) educational facilities (d) both a and b.

_____ 19. In the 1990s, private security employs (a) 50,000-100,000 (b) 100,000-500,000 (c) 500,000-1,000,000 (d) more than 1,000,000.

_____ 20. In the 1990s, employment in private security is expected to (a) increase (b) decrease (c) remain the same (d) fluctuate unpredictably.

Quiz Two   Name:_____

MODERN PRIVATE SECURITY: AN OVERVIEW

Select the one best answer for each of the following and put its letter in the blank to the left.

_____ 1. During the 1990s, the most employment gains will be made by (a) alarm companies (b) proprietary security officers (c) contractual security officers (d) private investigators.

_____ 2. Private security guards protect (a) individuals only (b) premises and property only (c) both a and b (d) neither a nor b.

_____ 3. Most private security officers spend the majority of their time (a) writing reports (b) performing non-enforcement functions (c) investigating crimes (d) apprehending criminals.

_____ 4. Security services that are provided by a firm or individual for a fee are called (a) proprietary services (b) contract services (c) special services (d) any of the preceding.

_____ 5. A survey conducted in 1990 found that (a) proprietary and contract staffs were about equal in size (b) contract security staffs greatly outnumbered proprietary security staffs (c) proprietary security staffs greatly outnumbered contract security staffs (d) the larger the security staff, the more likely it was to be contractual.

_____ 6. This same survey reported that security managers foresaw (a) an increase in proprietary services and a decrease in contractual services (b) a decrease in proprietary services and no change in contractual services (c) decreases in both proprietary and contractual services (d) increases in both proprietary and contractual services.

_____ 7. Advantages of proprietary security services include all except (a) lower cost (b) lower turn-over (c) greater knowledge of the operation (d) greater loyalty.

_____ 8. Advantages of contractual security services include all except (a) more flexibility (b) more objectivity (c) greater job security (d) better contracts with local law enforcement agencies.

_____ 9. The Employee Polygraph Protection Act (a) strictly regulated use of the polygraph for preemployment (b) does not apply to governmental agencies (c) allows use of the polygraph for preemployment screening by employers whose primary business is providing certain kinds of security services (d) all of the preceding.

_____ 10. The ASIS is (a) the American Society for Industrial Security (b) the American Society for Internal Security (c) the American Society of International Security (d) none of the preceding.

Quiz Two, page 2

_____ 11. To be a Certified Protection Professional, an individual must (a) join the Association of Protection Professionals (b) pass a written examination (c) have 10 years of experience (d) all of the preceding.

_____ 12. The mandatory subjects in the CPP examination include (a) legal aspects (b) loss prevention (c) substance abuse (d) all of the preceding.

_____ 13. A person is certified as a protection professional for (a) three years (b) four years (c) five years (d) life.

_____ 14. Proprietary security officers are (a) typically poorly trained (b) in-house or directly hired (c) continuously armed (d) all of the preceding.

_____ 15. The security function is the responsibility of (a) top management (b) every manager (c) both a and b (d) neither a nor b.

_____ 16. The Task Force on Private Security recommends that private security be regulated at the (a) federal level (b) regional level (c) state level (d) local level.

_____ 17. One requirement of a professional is (a) adherence to a code of ethics (b) an income above the national average (c) a college degree (d) all of the preceding.

_____ 18. The largest armed courier service is (a) Pinkerton's (b) Wackenhut (c) Loomis (d) Brink's.

_____ 19. The most frequently used type of private security personnel is (a) central alarm respondent (b) guard/patrol (c) armed courier (d) consultant.

_____ 20. The primary purpose of private security is to prevent losses caused by (a) human error (b) emergencies and disasters (c) criminal actions (d) all of the preceding.

Quiz Three Name: _____

THE PUBLIC/PRIVATE INTERFACE AND LEGAL AUTHORITY

Select the one best answer for each of the following and put its letter in the blank to the left.

_____ 1. The history of public policing and private security is (a) not relevant (b) intertwined (c) not of concern (d) seldom discussed.

_____ 2. More and more public life is nowadays conducted (a) in silence (b) on privately controlled property (c) in corporations (d) in business.

_____ 3. Policing in the past has been done under the auspices of (a) churches (b) peasants (c) workers (d) all of the preceding.

_____ 4. To determine whether policing is public or private it must be determined (a) who is paying for it (b) what its function is (c) who controls it (d) all of the preceding.

_____ 5. Private and public officers (a) have nothing in common (b) are at odds as to goals (c) have many things in common (d) do not and should not cooperate.

_____ 6. Public law enforcement officers (a) are profit oriented (b) serve specific clients (c) are hired by business (d) none of the preceding.

_____ 7. Private security officers (a) have police authority (b) have no police authority (c) are considered special police officers (d) none of the preceding.

_____ 8. Private security officers are restricted by (a) state statutes (b) criminal law (c) tort law (d) all of the preceding.

_____ 9. Some states give greater power to private police officers if they are (a) railroad officers (b) bank security officers (c) nuclear facilities officers (d) all of the preceding.

_____ 10. Employee pilferage is usually handled by (a) public police officers (b) private security officers (c) special investigators (d) none of the preceding.

_____ 11. Public police officers devote a large portion of their time to (a) enforcing laws (b) investigating crimes (c) apprehending suspects (d) all of the preceding.

_____ 12. The largest single problem in business and institutions is (a) murder (b) employee theft (c) assaults (d) none of the preceding.

_____ 13. Private security officers (a) work as U.S. marshals in federal court houses (b) guard military bases (c) guard public housing projects (d) all of the preceding.

_____ 14. In most instances, private police (a) do not have to give the Miranda warning (b) are bound by the Exclusionary Rule (c) cannot conduct searches without a warrant (d) all of the preceding.

Quiz Three, page 2

_____ 15. Privatization refers to the trend in which (a) private companies hire public police to perform specific duties (b) duties normally performed by public police officers are performed by private security officers (c) companies are keeping more and more information confidential (d) none of the preceding.

_____ 16. The right to command, enforce laws and compel obedience is (a) known as authority (b) known as power (c) not necessary for effective private security officers (d) a right reserved for only public police officers.

_____ 17. Power (a) relies on persuasion (b) lacks the support of law or rule (c) is the force used to carry out one's authority (d) all of the preceding.

_____ 18. A POST Commission is concerned with (a) Private Officers' Supplemental Training (b) Peace Officers' Standards and Training (c) Police Organizations' Successful Teamwork (d) Prevention of Officer Stress and Trauma.

_____ 19. Private security officers (a) have no more powers than private citizens (b) do have the power to arrest (c) may be authorized to conduct periodic inspections of personal items such as briefcases, purses and lunch boxes (d) all of the preceding.

_____ 20. Both public and private police strive to (a) prevent crime (b) apprehend law breakers (c) cooperate with the criminal justice system (d) all of the preceding.

Quiz Four   Name:_____

LEGAL LIABILITY

Select the one best answer for each of the following and put its letter in the blank to the left.

_____ 1. The largest indirect cost of economic crime has been the increase in (1) private security companies (b) police department personnel (c) civil litigation and damage awards (d) more security contracts.

_____ 2. The reason both judicial and legislative sanctions have been imposed on the security industry is (a) the improved quality of security services (b) the rising expectations of the public (c) the exceptional growth of the industry (d) all of the preceding.

_____ 3. The basis of law in the United States is the (a) common law (b) criminal law (c) civil law (d) case law.

_____ 4. A wrong against the public that the state prosecutes and seeks punishment for is known as (a) a tort (b) a crime (c) negligence (d) crime prevention.

_____ 5. The legal responsibility for the acts of another person because of some relationship with that person and whereby security officers are sued is known as (a) vicarious liability (b) joint liability (c) absolute liability (d) fixed liability.

_____ 6. An illegal act committed on purpose is known as (a) due process (b) a loss (c) an intentional wrong (d) collateral negligence.

_____ 7. The basic ingredient required for a civil lawsuit is (a) inadequate security (b) standard of care to protect (c) breach of duty causing harm (d) all of the preceding.

_____ 8. Respondent superior is the legal doctrine of master/servant which holds (a) the servant only is held liable for wrongful acts (b) the master only is held liable for wrongful acts (c) in certain cases the master is liable for the servant's actions (d) none of the preceding.

_____ 9. The degree of care a person of ordinary prudence would exercise in any similar circumstance in litigation is known as (a) standard of care (b) common sense (c) good judgment (d) all of the preceding.

_____ 10. The most common civil suits brought against private security officers are (a) assault (b) invasion of privacy (c) negligence (d) all of the preceding.

_____ 11. The unconsented, offensive touching of another person either directly or indirectly is known as (a) assault (b) battery (c) disorderly conduct (d) none of the preceding.

_____ 12. Many private security companies refuse to arm their security officers because (a) it requires too much gun training (b) it is too costly to purchase weapons (c) it involves too great a financial liability (d) none of the preceding.

_____ 13. An extremely important way for both proprietary and contractual security to reduce liability is to (a) hire trustworthy and qualified individuals (b) limit the amount of personnel in the agency (c) carry plenty of insurance (d) none of the preceding.

Quiz Four, page 2

_____ 14. A good liability protection system includes (a) discipline (b) policies and procedures (c) training (d) all of the preceding.

_____ 15. Security officers can help minimize lawsuits by (a) documenting their activities (b) keeping up on criminal and liability cases in the field (c) staying within the scope of the duties assigned (d) all of the preceding.

_____ 16. In any lawsuit, one of the most important documents to be discussed is (a) the contract (b) time sheets (c) salary schedule of security officers (d) indemnification.

_____ 17. Insurance companies treat private security agencies (a) with dignity (b) shabbily (c) positively, welcoming them with open arms (d) both a and c.

_____ 18. One area the insurance industry has virtually excluded from their policies when dealing with private security companies is (a) punitive damages (b) employee theft (c) reward funds (d) all of the preceding.

_____ 19. Where attorneys on both sides ask questions of a person involved in a lawsuit, and the questions and answers are recorded by a stenographer or court reporter, this is known as (a) examination (b) cross-examination (c) deposition (d) a mini-trial.

_____ 20. A civil wrong for which a person can be sued is known as (a) a felony (b) an intentional wrong (c) a tort (d) any of the preceding.

Quiz Five   Name:_____

ENHANCING SECURITY THROUGH PHYSICAL CONTROLS

Select the one best answer for each of the following and put its letter in the blank to the left.

_____ 1. A primary purpose of physical controls is to (a) deny access (b) discourage intruders (c) detect threats (d) all of the preceding.

_____ 2. CPTED refers to Crime Prevention Through (a) Environmental Design (b) Educational Development (c) Established Defense (d) Early Detection.

_____ 3. The <u>first</u> line of defense for an establishment may be the (a) perimeter of a facility (b) building exterior (c) building interior (d) any of the preceding.

_____ 4. The most frequently used security fencing is (a) concertina (b) chain link (c) razor ribbon (d) barbed wire.

_____ 5. An opening should be barred or screened if it is larger than (a) 24 square inches (b) 48 square inches (c) 96 square inches (d) 120 square inches.

_____ 6. A security lighting system to illuminate boundaries without glare would probably use (a) floodlights (b) street lights (c) fresnel units (d) shaded spot lights.

_____ 7. Illumination inside a guard house should be (a) less than that outside (b) the same as that outside (c) greater than that outside (d) any of the preceding, depending on the guard's function within the guard house.

_____ 8. When possible, the perimeter should have a clear zone of at least (a) five feet (b) ten feet (c) twenty feet (d) fifty feet.

_____ 9. Doors should have above them a minimum illumination of (a) 40 watts (b) 60 watts (c) 75 watts (d) 100 watts.

_____ 10. A common security risk in many modern buildings is the existence of (a) crawl spaces in the ceilings (b) warded locks (c) door transoms (d) both a and b.

_____ 11. Protection should be provided for any opening less than (a) five feet from the ground (b) ten feet from the ground (c) eighteen feet from the ground (d) all of the preceding.

_____ 12. Most safes are (a) fire resistant (b) burglar resistant (c) either a or b, but not both (d) both a and b.

_____ 13. The type of key-operated lock offering the best protection (a) has a deadbolt (b) is spring loaded (c) has a warded keyway (d) uses disc tumblers.

_____ 14. The <u>least</u> effective type of alarm is the (a) telephone-dialer (b) local alarm (c) central station alarm (d) police-connected alarm.

_____ 15. The simplest alarm sensors are (a) pressure devices (b) electro-mechanical devices (c) photoelectric devices (d) electro-magnetic devices.

Quiz Five, page 2

_____ 16. In the alarm most commonly used for point protection of a specified object requiring a high degree of security, the sensor detects (a) sound (b) electrical capacitance (c) vibration (d) motion.

_____ 17. The percentage of intrusion alarms that are false alarms is approximately (a) 70% (b) 80% (c) 90% (d) 95%.

_____ 18. The most frequent cause of false alarm is (a) faulty equipment (b) improper maintenance (c) outside short-wave transmission (d) user error.

_____ 19. Security managers should concentrate on (a) aesthetic needs (b) operational needs (c) safety and security needs (d) balancing all of the preceding.

_____ 20. Establishing and maintaining physical controls requires (a) attention to detail (b) limitless budget (c) specialized consultants (d) both a and b.

Quiz Six   Name:_____

ENHANCING SECURITY THROUGH PROCEDURAL CONTROLS

Select the one best answer for each of the following and put its letter in the blank to the left.

_____ 1. Another term for lost assets is (a) shrinkage (b) pilferage (c) theft (d) embezzlement.

_____ 2. Most experts agree that the single greatest cause of lost assets is (a) robbery (b) burglary (c) internal theft (d) carelessness.

_____ 3. The Employee Polygraph Protection Act prohibits employers from using lie detector tests for preemployment screening or during employment except for prospective employees of (a) private armored car firms (b) security alarm firms (c) security firms (d) all of the preceding.

_____ 4. For security purposes, it is best to limit the number of employees having access to (a) cash (b) valuable merchandise (c) storage areas (d) all of the preceding.

_____ 5. Keys should be given to (a) top management personnel (b) the chief custodian (c) only those whose jobs require it (d) both a and b.

_____ 6. It is best not to give entrance keys to (a) tenants of office buildings (b) custodians (c) the security director (d) both a and b.

_____ 7. Master keying (a) weakens security (b) has little effect on security (c) strengthens security (d) assures security.

_____ 8. Effective closing procedures include all <u>except</u> (a) turning off unneeded lights (b) locking all cash registers (c) locking all doors (d) checking all restrooms.

_____ 9. Security experts do not agree on whether (a) blinds or shades should be down or up at night (b) safes should be concealed or in plain view (c) master keying affects security or not (d) both a and b.

_____ 10. Access should be limited to (a) storage areas (b) the mail room (c) the duplicating room (d) all of the preceding.

_____ 11. Sound accounting procedures include all <u>except</u> (a) using prenumbered purchase orders (b) combining the purchasing and receiving functions (c) requiring vouchers for petty cash (d) centralized purchasing.

_____ 12. The receiving area should be (a) as close to the shipping area as possible (b) in an open, observable location (c) off-limits to all but suppliers' vehicles and company cars (d) all of the preceding.

_____ 13. The usual sequence of a business transaction is (a) purchasing department to receiving department to paying department (b) paying department to receiving department to purchasing department (c) purchasing department to paying department to receiving department (d) receiving department to paying department to purchasing department.

Quiz Six, page 2

_____ 14. *Blind receiving* is relying on (a) the packing slip (b) the purchase order (c) the bill of lading (d) any of the preceding.

_____ 15. A numbered metal seal bar is often used on (a) train boxcars (b) truck trailers (c) car trunks (d) both a and b.

_____ 16. For the best security, inventories should be taken (a) at least annually (b) at least semi-annually (c) monthly (d) continuously.

_____ 17. Providing employees with lockers (a) increases employees' security (b) decreases employer's security (c) both a and b (d) neither a nor b.

_____ 18. Insurance is one means of (a) eliminating risk (b) transferring risk (c) avoiding risk (d) any of the preceding.

_____ 19. The percent of losses caused by employees is estimated to be (a) 25% (b) 50% (c) 70% (d) 80%.

_____ 20. An employee who is caught stealing should be (a) reprimanded (b) fired and prosecuted (c) arrested and prosecuted (d) any of the preceding, depending on company policy.

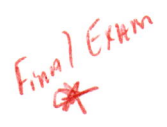

Quiz Seven   Final Exam   Name:_____

PREVENTING LOSS FROM ACCIDENTS AND EMERGENCIES

Select the one best answer for each of the following and put its letter in the blank to the left.

_____ 1. Preventing losses from accidents and emergencies, as far as a security manager is concerned, is (a) a critical responsibility (b) an unnecessary responsibility (c) an impossible responsibility (d) an OSHA responsibility.

_____ 2. Since the inception of OSHA, many security managers are also delegated responsibility for employees' (a) health (b) safety (c) honesty (d) both a and b.

_____ 3. OSHA has jurisdiction over any business with at least one employee and engaged in (a) federal contracts (b) state contracts (c) interstate commerce (d) both a and b.

_____ 4. The percent of accidents caused by human error (on or off the job) is approximately (a) 50% (b) 75% (c) 90% (d) 95%.

_____ 5. The fire triangle consist of all except (a) carbon dioxide (b) heat (c) fuel (d) oxygen.

_____ 6. Fires involving energized electrical installations are classified as Class (a) A (b) B (c) C (d) D.

_____ 7. The most common cause of industrial fire is related to (a) electrical shorts (b) carelessness (c) chemical actions (d) smoking.

_____ 8. The most sensitive fire detectors are (a) thermal (b) infrared (c) ionization (d) photoelectric.

_____ 9. The type of fire detector used is most homes is (a) thermal (b) photoelectric (c) ionization (d) infrared.

_____ 10. Type ABC extinguishers are effective against all except those fires involving (a) combustible metals (b) energized electrical appliances (c) flammable liquids (d) paper, wood or cloth.

_____ 11. Water is effective on fires involving (a) burning oil or gasoline (b) paper, wood or cloth (c) electrical appliances (d) both a and b.

_____ 12. If a sprinkler system is used, nothing should be stacked closer to it than (a) 8" (b) 12" (c) 18" (d) 24".

_____ 13. To protect against loss if a fire occurs (a) open windows and close doors (b) close windows and open doors (c) open both window and doors (d) close both windows and doors.

_____ 14. The first step to take should a fire occur is to (a) ground all elevators (b) close all doors (c) attempt to control the fire (d) call for help.

Quiz Seven, page 2

_____ 15. The type of fire occurring most frequently in computer rooms is Class (a) A (b) B (c) C (d) D.

_____ 16. For this item, select as many answers as are applicable in <u>your</u> situation. Natural disasters necessitating a contingency plan in <u>our</u> area include (a) floods (b) tornadoes (c) fires (d) earthquakes.

_____ 17. The percentage of bomb threats that are real is approximately (a) 2% (b) 5% (c) 10% (d) 25%.

_____ 18. When looking for a bomb, searchers should <u>not</u> (a) use portable radios (b) turn on lights (c) move rapidly (d) all of the preceding.

_____ 19. The appropriate clear zone around a suspected bomb is (a) 200' (b) 300' (c) 400' (d) 500'.

_____ 20. Procedures followed when evacuating due to a bomb threat include (a) closing doors and opening windows (b) opening doors and closing windows (c) opening both doors and windows (d) closing both doors and windows.

Quiz Eight   Name:_____

PREVENTING LOSSES FROM CRIMINAL ACTIONS

Select the one best answer for each of the following and put its letter in the blank to the left.

_____ 1. A tort is (a) a crime (b) a civil offense (c) either a or b (d) neither a nor b.

_____ 2. The specific conditions and/or actions that must exist to constitute a specific crime are called (a) elements (b) torts (c) evidence (d) facts.

_____ 3. A crime is an offense (a) against the state (b) against an individual (c) for which restitution is sought (d) all of the preceding.

_____ 4. A major source of information on crimes in the United States is (a) the *FBI Monitor* (b) *The Yearbook of Crime Statistics* (c) the Uniform Crime Reports (d) any of the preceding.

_____ 5. In most states shoplifting is classified as (a) larceny (b) theft (c) stealing (d) either a or b.

_____ 6. The basic difference between robbery and burglary is that in robbery (a) a weapon is used (b) force or threats are used (c) there is unlawful entry (d) the value of the property involved is greater.

_____ 7. The basic difference between larceny/theft and burglary is that in burglary (a) a weapon is used (b) there is unlawful entry (c) the value of the property is greater (d) any of the preceding.

_____ 8. The most common means of entrance into a building to commit burglary is (a) picking the lock (b) "hiding in" (c) using a duplicate key (d) prying open a door or window.

_____ 9. Most private security officers spend the majority of their time engaged in (a) investigating thefts (b) controlling personnel (c) performing non-crime-related functions (d) conducting security surveys.

_____ 10. Statutes defining major crimes such as murder and robbery (a) are uniform throughout the country (b) vary from state to state (c) vary from county to county (d) vary from city to city.

_____ 11. The most serious problem associated with robbery is (a) the potential for a hostage situation (b) the large amount of loss involved (c) the low probability of recovering the property (d) the inability of witnesses to identify the suspect.

_____ 12. The policy of not building up cash is a deterrent to (a) robbery (b) burglary (c) larceny/theft (d) any of the preceding.

_____ 13. Among the crimes that private security personnel may be called on to assist in preventing, the least likely is (a) assault (b) vandalism (c) trespassing (d) murder.

_____ 14. White-collar crime is (a) that committed by organized crime figures (b) that committed by professionals (c) business-related crime (d) computer-related crime.

Quiz Eight, page 2

_____ 15. The form of larceny/theft most often of prime concern to private security personnel is (a) embezzlement (b) credit card and check fraud (c) pilferage (d) insurance fraud.

_____ 16. According to FBI statistics, the fastest growing crime in the United States is (a) white-collar crime (b) arson (c) robbery (d) larceny/theft.

_____ 17. The key to effectively enforcing an employer's rights is to act (a) reasonably (b) forcefully (c) politely (d) swiftly.

_____ 18. Laws governing citizen's arrests are established by (a) the United States Constitution (b) federal statutes (c) state statutes (d) employment contracts.

_____ 19. An interrogation generally refers to the questioning of (a) a victim of a crime (b) a suspect in a crime (c) a witness to a crime (d) any of the preceding.

_____ 20. *Miranda v. Arizona* established the precedent that persons suspected of involvement in a crime (a) must be told of their rights prior to questioning by a public law enforcement officer (b) must be told of their rights prior to questioning by a private security officer (c) must not be questioned without a lawyer present (d) all of the preceding.

Quiz Nine   Name:_____

ENHANCING INFORMATION/COMPUTER SECURITY

Select the one best answer for each of the following and put its letter in the blank to the left.

_____ 1. A new breed of criminal and a new type of crime is becoming very prevalent because of (a) new knowledge (b) computers (c) automobiles (d) women in the work force.

_____ 2. Accessing a computer's database without authorization or exceeding authorization for the purpose of sabotage or fraud is known as (a) illegal monitoring (b) information access protection (c) a crime (d) legal monitoring.

_____ 3. The common acronym EDP means (a) electro-digital processing (b) each digital printout (c) early data posting (d) electronic data processing.

_____ 4. Technology that refers to "the burglar tool of the electronic age" is (a) microchips (b) minicassette recorders (c) eavesdropping microphones (d) computers.

_____ 5. Computer-related crime can involve (a) input data (b) output data (c) the program itself (d) all of the preceding.

_____ 6. Computerized banks are frequently the victim of (a) armed robbery (b) forgeries (c) check kiting (d) fraudulent loans.

_____ 7. The computer enthusiast who engages in electronic snooping is known as a (a) dork (b) junkie (c) jumper (d) hacker.

_____ 8. Pirating software, including video games, is a violation of the (a) patent laws (b) copyright laws (c) common law (d) corporate sense of fair play.

_____ 9. A common hazard in storing computer tapes is (a) heat (b) humidity (c) magnets (d) all of the preceding.

_____ 10. By passing laws to plug the loopholes that prohibit traditional theft by computer, states have tightened their (a) traffic codes (b) criminal laws (c) common law (d) business law.

_____ 11. The Electronic Communications Privacy Act of 1986 was passed to (a) protect the privacy of high-tech communications (b) prevent unauthorized access to computers (c) prevent exceeding authorization of access to a computer (d) all of the preceding.

_____ 12. Most computer crimes are discovered by (a) auditors (b) chance (c) security personnel (d) guards.

_____ 13. An effective administrative control used by companies who hire computer personnel is (a) a polygraph examination (b) pencil and paper test (c) background investigation (d) all of the preceding.

_____ 14. According to surveys, the percentage of computer crimes that are detected is (a) 1% (b) 3% (c) 5% (d) 50%.

Quiz Nine, page 2

_____ 15. Some computer crime can be blamed on (a) dishonest computers (b) employees (c) faulty software (d) all of the preceding.

_____ 16. Programs of instruction that tell computers what to do are known as (a) hardware (b) software (c) videoware (d) firmware.

_____ 17. Violation of the Electronic Communications Act of 1986 is a (a) felony (b) misdemeanor (c) gross misdemeanor (d) petty misdemeanor.

_____ 18. A logical control that restricts access to a computer may be a (a) telephone number (b) key (c) supervisor's permission (d) password.

_____ 19. Administrative control that establishes someone who is responsible for an act is known as (a) supervision (b) chain of command (c) accountability (d) all of the preceding.

_____ 20. The chances of a computer criminal being caught and going to jail are (a) 1 in 200 (b) 1 in 2,700 (c) 1 in 10,000 (d) 1 in 27,000.

Quiz Ten   Name:_____

ENHANCING PUBLIC RELATIONS

Select the one best answer for each of the following and put its letter in the blank to the left.

_____ 1. Public relations as part of the private security officer's job can best be described as (a) vital (b) routine (c) regular (d) general.

_____ 2. The private security officer can best understand the problems of business through (a) experience (b) education (c) training (d) role playing.

_____ 3. The most important influence on the private security officer's image is (a) television shows (b) newspaper stories (c) movies (d) everyday contacts.

_____ 4. The physical appearance of the private security officer adds to (a) bigotry (b) difficulties (c) totalitarianism (d) authoritarianism.

_____ 5. One key to enhancing public relations is using (a) impartiality (b) sympathy (c) cynicism (d) suspiciousness.

_____ 6. Public relations is (a) not necessary (b) a planned program of policies (c) expensive (d) both a and b.

_____ 7. The attitude of most businesses and organizations toward public relations is (a) not concerned (b) very important (c) of minor concern (d) both b and c.

_____ 8. Public relations (a) bolsters an image (b) creates good will (c) creates good interpersonal relationships (d) all of the preceding.

_____ 9. When a company requires a highly visible security presence the best type of uniform is (a) the soft look (b) the military look (c) the police look (d) unimportant.

_____ 10. To act professionally, the private security officer must (a) be noncommittal (b) enforce rules rigidly (c) have a positive attitude (d) be non-communicative.

_____ 11. The greatest service provided a customer by a security guard is (a) giving directions (b) deterring crime (c) interviewing persons (d) looking official.

_____ 12. One controversial piece of equipment that security companies usually discourage is (a) mace (b) clubs (c) whistles (d) guns.

_____ 13. The emphasis with all modern private security uniforms should be (a) practicality (b) ease of maintenance (c) suitability for site requirements (d) all of the preceding.

_____ 14. Properly designed and properly worn uniforms (a) enhance the self-image of the officer (b) enhance the image of the employer (c) enhance security for the company (d) all of the preceding.

_____ 15. One disadvantage of the military uniform is that it (a) resembles a police uniform (b) has brass buttons (c) looks professional (d) gives a highly visible presence.

Quiz Ten, page 2

_____ 16. Security officers whose assignments are in institutions where public trust is essential must be (a) well recognized (b) highly visible (c) considerate (d) all of the preceding.

_____ 17. Private security image is the result of (a) good daily contacts (b) the behavior of the private security officer (c) personal appearance (d) all of the preceding.

_____ 18. When a visitor intrudes into a restricted area of a company, the security officer should (a) place the person under arrest (b) draw his gun and threaten the visitor (c) explain the situation to the visitor and escort him out (d) call the local police department.

_____ 19. If security officers are to be effective on the job they must (a) be trained (b) be informed of the company's policies (c) know what is expected of them (d) all of the preceding.

_____ 20. When security officers must intervene in a situation they should be (a) objective (b) emotional (c) biased (d) all of the preceding.

Quiz Eleven   Name:_____

THE INVESTIGATIVE FUNCTION ✱ Final Exam

Select the one best answer for each of the following and put its letter in the blank to the left.

_____ 1. The word *investigation* comes from the word(s) (a) *investia* (b) *pater nostre* (c) *vestigar* (d) *garevesti*.

_____ 2. Video surveillance is valuable to find out whether (a) a crime is being committed (b) safety violations are occurring (c) armed robbers can be identified (d) all of the preceding.

_____ 3. When an accident occurs involving injury to an employee, one of the most important involvements in the investigation should be by (a) another employee (b) the security officer (c) the public police (d) senior management.

_____ 4. When conduct creates a workplace environment that a reasonable person would find hostile and abusive, this could be construed to constitute (a) a felony (b) sexual harassment (c) normal conduct (d) acceptable conduct.

_____ 5. Criminal investigations conducted by security officers usually are different in that they (a) usually involve employees (b) involve hardened criminals (c) center around persons with criminal records (d) invariably involve criminal prosecution.

_____ 6. It is well known that companies prefer private security officers investigating uncovered incidents because they are (a) less embarrassing to the company (b) more expedient (c) less expensive (d) all of the preceding.

_____ 7. The investigation of a total set of circumstances by a security officer, that leads the officer to believe that an offense has occurred is known as (a) probable cause (b) prediction (c) predication (d) reasonable cause.

_____ 8. Effective investigations require the officers to (a) use an organized approach (b) take their time (c) find the facts (d) all of the preceding.

_____ 9. If you were conducting an investigation and needed someone to examine some official papers for you, you would likely seek out a (a) serologist (b) microscopic consultant (c) forensic document examiner (d) all of the preceding.

_____ 10. One of the most important inquiries a security officer should make when investigating an assault is to obtain (a) complete descriptions of any weapons (b) details of the incident (c) complete description of the suspect(s) (d) all of the preceding.

_____ 11. Crimes such as shoplifting, purse snatching and pick pocketing are categorized as (a) theft (b) minor crimes (c) nuisance crimes (d) breaches of peace.

_____ 12. A harmful act whereby the usefulness or value of property is destroyed or considerably diminished is known as (a) bigotry (b) vandalism (c) fair value theft (d) all of the preceding.

Quiz Eleven, page 2

_____ 13. The primary characteristic of an investigator is (a) inquisitiveness (b) objectivity (c) efficiency (d) indifference.

_____ 14. The single most important factor in determining the successful disposition of an incident is (a) vigilant surveillance (b) background information provided by the property owner (c) the information gathered by the security officer at the time of the initial report (d) the involvement of the public police.

_____ 15. Investigative personnel are concerned with (a) the truth or falsity of statements (b) crimes and wrongdoings (c) preemployment background checks (d) all of the preceding.

_____ 16. Investigators involved in the new field of computer forensics are called (a) floppy cops (b) the net patrol (c) disk detectives (d) cybercops.

_____ 17. Public records that private security investigators have ready access to are (a) birth records (b) mortgages (c) liens and judgments (d) all of the preceding.

_____ 18. In the law of domestic relations the claims of the aggrieved must be (a) reliable (b) credible (c) candid (d) all of the preceding.

_____ 19. Crime is very important to the private security officer because it means (a) increased business insurance costs (b) reduced profits (c) loss of investor equity (d) all of the preceding.

_____ 20. Some areas a private security officer will look into when doing a background investigation for preemployment screening are (a) use of drugs (b) heredity (c) religious beliefs (d) all of the preceding.

Quiz Twelve   1-8-06 Quiz   Final Exam   Name:_____

OBTAINING AND PROVIDING INFORMATION

Select the one best answer for each of the following and put its letter in the blank to the left.

_____ 1. Notes should not be recorded in (a) ink (b) pencil (c) notebooks (d) both b and c.

_____ 2. To verify spellings and numbers (a) repeat the information (b) write legibly (c) print (d) all of the preceding.

_____ 3. Reports dealing with the routine functioning of the business or agency are called (a) administrative (b) operational (c) formal (d) informal.

_____ 4. A statement which can be proven true is called (a) a statement (b) an inference (c) a fact (d) a judgment.

_____ 5. Statements that can be discussed reasonably include (a) opinions (b) inferences (c) facts (d) both b and c.

_____ 6. If a report is objective, it is (a) opinionated (b) fair (c) partial (d) all of the preceding.

_____ 7. The emotional overtones of a word are called (a) positive (b) negative (c) connotations (d) denotations.

_____ 8. A report which includes only one side of the story is (a) impartial (b) slanted (c) objective (d) both a and b.

_____ 9. To be complete, a report should answer the questions (a) who and what (b) where and when (c) why and how (d) all of the preceding.

_____ 10. A report can be made less wordy by (a) leaving out unnecessary information (b) including only one side of the story (c) using abbreviations (d) both a and c.

_____ 11. A sentence that does not contain empty words is (a) The 6'2" man fled north on State Street. (b) The car is blue in color. (c) Despite the fact that he was given a warning, he ran. (d) He was born in the month of April.

_____ 12. Clarity can be obtained by (a) keeping descriptive words and phrases close to the words they modify (b) using abbreviations (c) organizing thoughts into lengthy sentences (d) both a and c.

_____ 13. In writing, mechanics refers to the rules for (a) spelling (b) capitalization (c) punctuation (d) all of the preceding.

_____ 14. An example of nonstandard English is (a) He was goin' home. (b) The lite was brite. (c) He seen the dog. (d) all of the preceding.

_____ 15. If a person has very poor handwriting, he or she should (a) type reports (b) print reports (c) use cursive writing (d) either a or b.

Quiz Twelve, page 2

_____ 16. Nonverbal communications includes (a) touch (b) eyes (c) posture (d) all of the preceding.

_____ 17. The one critical aspect in the security officer's work is (a) accuracy (b) shined shoes (c) punctuality (d) wearing a tie.

_____ 18. Good notes help security officers (a) remember incidents (b) remember actions they took (c) remember conditions (d) all of the preceding.

_____ 19. Empathy means (a) where the other person is coming from (b) categorical (c) sarcasm (d) avoidance.

_____ 20. Statements about the unknown based on the known are referred to as (a) superstitions (b) inferences (c) opinions (d) any of the preceding.

Quiz Thirteen   Name:_____

TESTIFYING IN COURT

Select the one best answer for each of the following and put its letter in the blank to the left.

_____ 1. One word that strikes fear into the hearts of many security officers and their employers is (a) ineffective (b) liability (c) progressive (d) proprietary.

_____ 2. Appearance, behavior and attitude in court are (a) not important (b) somewhat important (c) very important (d) irrelevant.

_____ 3. When a security officer is called in for a deposition, in reality it is like (a) a criminal interrogation (b) being questioned by the police (c) a police lineup (d) a mini-trial.

_____ 4. The first sequence of events in a criminal trial is (a) prediction of the verdict (b) instructions to the jury (c) picking the jury (d) calling the case from the court docket.

_____ 5. Usually a private security officer's testimony in court will be called into question by the (a) defense attorney (b) prosecuting attorney (c) judge (d) either a or b.

_____ 6. To "impeach a witness" in court is to (a) ask them to resign (b) imply that they are lying (c) discredit their testimony (d) any of the preceding.

_____ 7. When testifying in court, security officers should not (a) refer to the judge as "Your Honor" (b) state that the suspect is guilty (c) refer to their notes (d) both b and c.

_____ 8. It is acceptable behavior for a security officer to (a) review the case with the prosecutor before it goes to court (b) use notes while testifying in court (c) ask for a complex question to be broken down (d) any of the preceding.

_____ 9. Private security officers' reports and their testimony in court reflect their (a) intelligence (b) education (c) professionalism (d) all of the preceding.

_____ 10. Hearsay in a court of law is (a) relevant (b) admissible (c) inadmissible (d) both a and b.

_____ 11. Testifying in court is like shooting a weapon in that it happens only once in awhile. Therefore you should (b) be prepared to use vulgarities (b) be correct and accurate (c) memorize all your notes all the time (d) all of the preceding.

_____ 12. Attorneys try to cast doubt on your testimony by (a) using rapid-fire questioning (b) attacking your investigative skills (c) being intimidatingly rude (d) all of the preceding.

_____ 13. The formula for successful courtroom testimony is to be (a) brief (b) polite (c) emphatic (d) all of the preceding.

_____ 14. To be an expert in any field, one must have (a) the experience (b) formal education (c) written articles or textbooks on the subject (d) all of the preceding.

Quiz Thirteen, page 2

_____ 15. The initial questioning of a witness or defendant by a lawyer who is using the person's testimony to further his or her case is known as (a) direct examination (b) cross-examination (c) privileged communications (d) qualifying the witness.

_____ 16. The purpose of cross-examination is to (a) assess the validity of the testimony (b) lay the ground work for a hung jury (c) see if the jurors are paying attention (d) all of the preceding.

_____ 17. The jury interprets the nervousness of a security officer on the witness stand to mean (a) he's lying (b) he's inexperienced (c) he's hiding something (d) none of the preceding.

_____ 18. As a security officer, you will be testifying in a court of law because you have (a) hearsay evidence (b) personal knowledge of the case (c) opinions (d) any of the preceding.

_____ 19. When a jury can't render a verdict in a case, it is known as (a) a hung jury (b) jury malpractice (c) contempt (d) an ex parte jury.

_____ 20. One of the most effective ways of testifying and creating an efficient image in the courtroom is to (a) rephrase meaningful questions (b) appear aloof (c) concentrate on the questions asked (d) get angry, showing your concern and vested interest.

Quiz Fourteen   Name:_____

LOSS PREVENTION THROUGH RISK MANAGEMENT

Select the one best answer for each of the following and put its letter in the blank to the left.

_____ 1. The potential for injury, damage or loss with no possible benefit is (a) simple risk (b) complex risk (c) pure risk (d) dynamic risk.

_____ 2. Accepting credit card purchases is an example of (a) simple risk (b) complex risk (c) pure risk (d) dynamic risk.

_____ 3. Credit card fraud is an example of (a) simple risk (b) complex risk (c) pure risk (d) dynamic risk.

_____ 4. Risk management focuses on (a) anticipating risks (b) appraising risks (c) taking action to reduce risk (d) all of the preceding.

_____ 5. Effective risk management is not (a) costly (b) crisis-oriented (c) systematic (d) all of the preceding.

_____ 6. The first step in risk management is usually (a) policy formation (b) risk analysis (c) specification of a protection plan (d) education of all employees.

_____ 7. The most important factor in risk analysis is (a) vulnerability (b) probability (c) criticality (d) a, b and c equally.

_____ 8. Establishing vulnerability involves (a) identifying threats (b) analyzing those factors that favor loss (c) determining the consequences of possible losses (d) all of the preceding.

_____ 9. A security survey is (a) a questionnaire completed by all employees (b) a questionnaire completed by top management (c) an on-site analysis of the existing security system (d) both a and b.

_____ 10. Security surveys are put into the form of (a) a check-list (b) a diagram (c) an outline (d) any of the preceding.

_____ 11. The only risks that can be completely eliminated are (a) dynamic risks (b) pure risks (c) simple risks (d) none of the preceding.

_____ 12. When it is realistic to do so, the best alternative is (a) risk transfer (b) risk elimination (c) risk reduction (d) risk acceptance.

_____ 13. Implementing check-cashing policies is an example of (a) risk transfer (b) risk elimination (c) risk reduction (d) risk acceptance.

_____ 14. Installing an alarm system is an example of (a) risk transfer (b) risk elimination (c) risk reduction (d) risk acceptance.

_____ 15. Carrying insurance is an example of (a) risk transfer (b) risk elimination (c) risk reduction (d) risk acceptance.

Quiz Fourteen, page 2

_____ 16. Raising prices to cover losses is an example of (a) risk transfer (b) risk elimination (c) risk reduction (d) risk acceptance.

_____ 17. If the cost for security exceeds the potential for loss, the best alternative is (a) risk transfer (b) risk elimination (c) risk reduction (d) risk acceptance.

_____ 18. Risk spreading is closely related to (a) risk transfer (b) risk elimination (c) risk reduction (d) risk acceptance.

_____ 19. The total security system should be evaluated (a) daily (b) monthly (c) semi-annually (d) annually.

_____ 20. When security managers are planning a security system, budget should be (a) of greatest concern (b) of much importance (c) of some concern (d) of little consequence.

Quiz Fifteen Name:_____

INDUSTRIAL SECURITY

Select the one best answer for each of the following and put its letter in the blank to the left.

_____ 1. Security officers were first used in manufacturing to guard against (a) sabotage (b) espionage (c) theft (d) both a and b.

_____ 2. One of the most serious areas of industrial loss is (a) tools (b) machinery (c) supplies (d) uniforms.

_____ 3. The word *sabotage* is derived from the French word *sabot*, meaning (a) destroy (b) injure (c) machinery (d) shoes.

_____ 4. Espionage refers to (a) theft of trade secrets (b) work stoppages (c) destruction of machinery (d) any of the preceding.

_____ 5. Security in manufacturing plants became much more prevalent as a result of (a) increasing strikes (b) the world wars (c) the formation of unions (d) the formation of OSHA.

_____ 6. Security needs are usually greater in (a) steel mills (b) furniture factories (c) general merchandising warehouses (d) both a and b.

_____ 7. Security needs generally increase as (a) the size of the plant increases (b) the number of key executives increases (c) profits increase (d) all of the preceding.

_____ 8. Compared to other types of businesses, in industry, internal theft is (a) not a real problem (b) less of a problem (c) equally prevalent (d) more prevalent.

_____ 9. Valuable side products might include (a) metal shavings (b) wood scraps (c) food scraps (d) any of the preceding.

_____ 10. Tool loss can be reduced by instituting (a) a check-in/out procedure (b) an identification system (c) periodic inspections (d) all of the preceding.

_____ 11. If an employee breaks a tool, the employee should (a) pay for it (b) turn it in (c) replace it (d) both a and b.

_____ 12. Most cargo thefts involve collusion between (a) employees (b) employees and outside individuals (c) employers and employees (d) truck drivers and organized crime.

_____ 13. Pilferage in industry commonly includes (a) maintenance supplies (b) gasoline (c) uniforms (d) any of the preceding.

_____ 14. Items that not only can be stolen, but also can assist a thief, include (a) scrap metal (b) metal detectors (c) hand trucks (d) any of the preceding.

_____ 15. Proper maintenance of tools is important because it (a) avoids damaging merchandise (b) reduces production slowdowns (c) lengthens the tool's life (d) all of the preceding.

Quiz Fifteen, page 2

_____ 16. Most cargo thefts involve vehicles that (a) belong to the company (b) are authorized to be in the area (c) are stolen (d) both a and b.

_____ 17. Effective means of reducing cargo theft include all except (a) preloading trucks (b) using factory-sealed cartons (c) sealing truck trailer doors (d) making non-stop hauls.

_____ 18. The great majority of cargo theft losses result from (a) hijacking (b) unexplained losses (c) internal theft (d) breaking and entering.

_____ 19. The seal system is commonly used on (a) railway cars (b) truck trailers (c) airplanes (d) both a and b.

_____ 20. Over 40 states allow broad police powers to security officers working in (a) financial institutions (b) the railroad industry (c) the airline industry (d) all of the preceding.

Quiz Sixteen   Name:_____

RETAIL SECURITY

Select the one best answer for each of the following and put its letter in the blank to the left.

_____ 1. Retail businesses that absorb the greatest losses from thefts are (a) food stores (b) drug stores (c) general merchandising stores (d) record shops.

_____ 2. The most frequent crime against retail establishments is (a) bad checks (b) vandalism (c) employee theft (d) shoplifting.

_____ 3. In many states, price-changing is a form of (a) shoplifting (b) larceny (c) both a and b (d) neither a nor b.

_____ 4. A great majority of shoplifting is done by (a) ordinary customers (b) kleptomaniacs (c) professionals (d) vagrants.

_____ 5. A booster box has a hinged (a) top (b) bottom (c) end (d) any of the preceding.

_____ 6. The most effective deterrent to shoplifting is alert, well-trained (a) security officers (b) floorwalkers (c) sales people (d) supervisors.

_____ 7. Floorwalkers are (a) prevention-oriented (b) apprehension-oriented (c) both a and b (d) neither a nor b.

_____ 8. Typewriters can be protected from theft by (a) loop alarms (b) cable alarms (c) ribbon switch alarms (d) any of the preceding.

_____ 9. *People v. Zelinski* established that the Exclusionary Rule applies to private security officers (a) acting in a "public" capacity (b) working in buildings open to the public (c) working directly with the public (d) all of the preceding.

_____ 10. A study of apprehended shoplifters in Cook County, Illinois, found that the best deterrent to repeated offenses was (a) stiff penalties (b) special courts (c) neither a nor b (d) both a and b.

_____ 11. In many states, prima facie evidence of the intent to shoplift is (a) concealment (b) clothes with many pockets (c) carrying empty shopping bags (d) any of the preceding.

_____ 12. Of all checks cashed in the United States, the percentage that are cashed in retail stores is approximately (a) 50% (b) 80% (c) 90% (d) 95%.

_____ 13. Heaviest losses from bad checks are sustained by (a) supermarkets (b) department stores (c) liquor stores (d) gas stations.

_____ 14. High-risk checks include all except (a) second-party checks (b) payroll checks (c) counter checks (d) post-dated checks.

_____ 15. Writing a bad check is classified as (a) forgery (b) fraud (c) embezzlement (d) either a or b.

Quiz Sixteen, page 2

_____ 16. A common type of bad check is (a) forged (b) no-account (c) insufficient funds (d) all of the preceding.

_____ 17. Acceptable identification for check-cashing purposes would be (a) military I.D. (b) birth certificate (c) social security card (d) any of the preceding.

_____ 18. Experience shows that the majority of returned personal checks are numbered under (a) 100 (b) 300 (c) 500 (d) 1000.

_____ 19. The "popular" salesperson (a) is an asset to a retail store (b) should be investigated (c) should be transferred to another department (d) both a and b.

_____ 20. The honesty of sales personnel who handle cash is often tested by using (a) a shopping service (b) a service shopper (c) floorwalkers (d) any of the preceding.

Quiz Seventeen   Name:_____

COMMERCIAL SECURITY

Select the one best answer for each of the following and put its letter in the blank to the left.

_____ 1. A major security problem in office buildings is (a) regulation and control of visitor traffic (b) vandalism (c) credit card theft (d) all of the preceding.

_____ 2. Office building security relies most heavily upon (a) alarms (b) access control (c) locks (d) security officers.

_____ 3. The core concept places in an office building's center (a) the elevators (b) the restrooms (c) the service facilities (d) all of the preceding.

_____ 4. Theft of hotel/motel property may be reduced by (a) luggage checks (b) key control (c) not identifying the property (d) any of the preceding.

_____ 5. Federal regulations have been passed regarding security in (a) banks (b) airports (c) hotels/motels (d) both a and b.

_____ 6. At the heart of hotel/motel security is (a) an alarm system (b) house detectives (c) key control (d) a secure vault.

_____ 7. Financial institutions' losses are greatest from (a) robbery (b) burglary (c) larceny (d) vandalism.

_____ 8. Prior to the Bank Protection Act, most financial institutions relied for their security on (a) alarms (b) surveillance cameras (c) security guards (d) all of the preceding.

_____ 9. The Bank Protection Act sets up security requirements for all (a) federally insured financial institutions (b) financial institutions that deal across state lines (c) savings and loan institutions (d) all of the preceding.

_____ 10. Given the requirements of the Bank Protection Act, it is likely that the security equipment installed to meet the requirements is now approximately (a) 5 years old (b) 10 years old (c) 20 years old (d) 35 years old.

_____ 11. Use of "bait money" involves (a) recording the serial numbers (b) marking the bills (c) positioning the money so as to set off an alarm if it is removed (d) all of the preceding.

_____ 12. According to Green, the future of security in high-rise apartment buildings and housing complexes offers (a) great potential (b) average potential (c) limited potential (d) no potential.

_____ 13. In making hotels and motels more convenient for guests, management has increased their vulnerability to (a) theft (b) vandalism (c) assault (d) all of the preceding.

_____ 14. The number of states requiring sprinklers in hotel rooms is approximately (a) 5 (b) 15 (c) 24 (d) 35.

Quiz Seventeen, page 2

_____ 15. The Hotel-Motel Fire Safety Act requires that by 1996 federal employees who stay or meet in hotel rooms must do so in establishments that have sprinkler systems if they are more than (a) two stories (b) three stories (c) five stories (d) eight stories.

_____ 16. The primary means to reduce problems at public gatherings is (a) surveillance systems (b) security personnel (c) uniformed police officers (d) undercover police officers.

_____ 17. Shirley suggested improving security at public event ticket windows by creating a buffer zone around the window of (a) 10-20 feet (b) 25-50 feet (c) 50-75 feet (d) 75-100 feet.

_____ 18. A *unique* security problem at racetracks is (a) crowd control (b) parking security (c) controlling phone calls prior to post times (d) alcohol control.

_____ 19. The FAA requires (a) a sworn law enforcement officer within five minutes of all screening points (b) installation of security surveillance equipment (c) use of metal detectors at all screening points (d) all of the preceding.

_____ 20. People who use a mass transit system are most often victimized (a) on the way to or from the station (b) at the station entrance or exit (c) in the station (d) on the conveyance.

Quiz Eighteen   Name:_____

INSTITUTIONAL SECURITY

Select the one best answer for each of the following and put its letter in the blank to the left.

_____ 1. The criminal problem most frequently encountered in fine arts museums is (a) vandalism (b) arson (c) theft (d) assault.

_____ 2. The chance of recovering a stolen art treasure is less than (a) 1% (b) 5% (c) 10% (d) 20%.

_____ 3. According to the president of the International Association of Art Security, the most important defense against well-organized art theft is (a) a centralized, computerized record of all valuable works (b) well-trained security officers (c) a comprehensive alarm system (d) a comprehensive CCTV system that is continuously monitored.

_____ 4. In the ARTCENTRAL system, all works of art are (a) visibly labeled (b) invisibly labeled (c) recorded by photogrammetry (d) all of the preceding.

_____ 5. A survey of attendees at a campus security conference identified their primary security concern to be (a) vandalism (b) access control (c) theft (d) safety.

_____ 6. A major problem for security in hospitals is (a) emergency rooms (b) waiting rooms (c) elevators (d) all of the preceding.

_____ 7. In a survey of almost 200 hospitals, the most formidable security problem indicated was (a) violence in the emergency room (b) theft of narcotics (c) possibility of fire (d) visitor control.

_____ 8. The item most frequently stolen in hospitals is (a) drugs (b) linens (c) food (d) office supplies.

_____ 9. Public school systems face security problems including (a) vandalism (b) crimes of violence (c) burglary (d) all of the preceding.

_____ 10. *In re T.L.O.* held that school officials and teachers (a) have an unlimited right to search students (b) must have reasonable grounds to search students (c) must have probable cause to search students (d) cannot search students.

_____ 11. According to Green, campus security has been evolving from (a) high visibility to low visibility (b) low visibility to high visibility (c) uniformed to nonuniformed (d) nonuniformed to uniformed.

_____ 12. Major losses in libraries result from (a) vandalism (b) theft or damage to books (c) electronic marking (d) all of the preceding.

_____ 13. Major security problems of museums and art galleries include (a) theft (b) fraud (c) arson (d) all of the preceding.

Quiz Eighteen, page 2

_____ 14. The last line of defense for individual pieces of art is usually (a) fixed-point alarm (b) volumetric alarm (c) locks (d) security personnel.

_____ 15. According to the Metropolitan Police Department, Washington, DC, the amount of church, synagogue and temple crime reported is (a) one-fourth (b) one-third (c) one-half (d) unknown.

_____ 16. Increases in crime against religious property and personnel have been seen in (a) burglary and robbery (b) assault (c) vandalism and arson (d) all of the preceding.

_____ 17. The majority of states have legislation providing police authority for proprietary security personnel (a) in hospitals (b) on college campuses (c) in art museums (d) in public libraries.

_____ 18. The type of facility most likely to experience a fire is a(n) (a) hospital (b) educational institution (c) art gallery (d) museum.

_____ 19. One of the fastest growing fields in the security industry is (a) hospital security (b) library security (c) art gallery security (d) museum security.

_____ 20. Vandalism is a major security concern in (a) museums (b) educational institutions (c) art galleries (d) all of the preceding.

Quiz Nineteen   Name:_____

OTHER APPLICATIONS OF SECURITY AT WORK

Select the one best answer for each of the following and put its letter in the blank to the left.

_____ 1. One area where little attention has been given as far as security for the patron is concerned is (a) parking lots and ramp areas (b) neighborhood safety (c) school grounds (d) none of the preceding.

_____ 2. Personal protection in foreign countries can be enhanced if (a) the language is known (b) the political atmosphere is known (c) the culture is understood (d) all of the preceding.

_____ 3. Security problems that involve courtroom security are (a) potential assaults (b) witnesses not showing up (c) unruly spectators (d) both a and c.

_____ 4. One of the most effective crime prevention tools for parking lots and ramps is (a) blacktopping (b) lights (c) unlighted areas (d) any of the preceding.

_____ 5. Effectiveness of executive protection depends on (a) having plenty of bodyguards (b) having a bullet-resistant automobile (c) family members keeping a low profile (d) using escort services at all times.

_____ 6. Terrorism around the world (a) is on the rise (b) seems to be diminishing (c) is no longer a concern for governments (d) is about the same as it was 10 years ago.

_____ 7. Court security must be (a) vigilant (b) effective (c) inoffensive (d) all of the preceding.

_____ 8. Federal trials that require a high degree of security in the courtroom are those dealing with (a) embezzlement (b) misappropriation of federal funds (c) drugs (d) security fraud.

_____ 9. Parking garages always have been the favorite movie setting for depicting (a) chases (b) assaults (c) kidnappings (d) all of the preceding.

_____ 10. Parking garages and ramps make people uneasy about walking through to pick up their vehicles because of (a) poor lighting in many instances (b) blind spots (c) the many hiding places (d) all of the preceding.

_____ 11. When owners or lessees fail to uphold their responsibilities in parking ramp management, they could be (a) faced with possible litigation (b) left to fend for themselves (c) left alone to manage as they see fit (d) none of the preceding.

_____ 12. Some crimes patrons of parking lots might be exposed to are (a) theft (b) robbery (c) assault (d) all of the preceding.

_____ 13. To improve parking lot management, the managers must (a) sell the lot or garage (b) assess the situation (c) stay neutral and let things happen on their natural course (d) maintain a status quo attitude.

Quiz Nineteen, page 2

_____ 14. The single weakness of human patrols in parking lots or parking ramps is that they (a) lack responsibility (b) can be in only one area at a time (c) lack dedication (d) may fall asleep.

_____ 15. Most people view citations (a) as a good lesson in parking (b) with a complimentary attitude (c) as a form of punishment (d) with a nonchalant attitude.

_____ 16. Prohibited items that may not be brought into the courtroom are (a) wallets (b) small change (c) weapons (d) all of the preceding.

_____ 17. Most disruptions caused in the courtroom are attributed to (a) males 21-35 (b) females 21-35 (c) teenagers (d) transvestites.

_____ 18. To curtail security problems in the courtroom, officers use (a) metal detectors (b) surveillance equipment (c) x-ray machines (d) all of the preceding.

_____ 19. The level of security required to protect a political candidate depends on (a) the type of office sought (b) the finances available (c) the personnel available (d) an educated guess.

_____ 20. The most common way that criminals prey on executives is (a) blackmail (b) extortions (c) assaults (d) harassment.

Quiz Twenty   Name:_____

THE CHALLENGES OF VIOLENCE IN THE WORKPLACE

Select the one best answer for each of the following and put its letter in the blank to the left.

_____ 1. Over what percentage of crime victimization incidents in the workplace are never reported to police? (a) 5% (b) 15% (c) 50% (d) 75%

_____ 2. Attacks upon employees can result from (a) irrational behavior (b) interpersonal conflict (c) dissatisfaction with service (d) all of the preceding.

_____ 3. The fastest growing type of homicide in this country today is (a) murder on the streets (b) murder in the workplace (c) capital punishment (d) spousal murder.

_____ 4. Violence in the workplace affects (a) morale (b) employee confidence (c) employee productivity (d) all of the preceding.

_____ 5. When putting together an incident management team, the following people should not be considered (a) security (b) legal counsel (c) human resources division (d) all should be on the team.

_____ 6. Violence-induced injury in the workplace carries with it (a) serious financial implications (b) little legal liability (c) promotions or pay raises for those who report it (d) the opportunity to cleanse the premises of type A personalities.

_____ 7. To make the workplace safer, employees must have (a) legal responsibility (b) moral responsibility (c) a good faith effort (d) all of the preceding.

_____ 8. One in four perpetrators of workplace violence is (a) suicidal (b) mentally incompetent (c) handicapped (d) highly intelligent.

_____ 9. Preventive measures toward workplace violence include (a) employee education (b) preemployment screening (c) drug testing (d) all of the preceding.

_____ 10. Once a company is struck by violence in the workplace (a) it will never recover (b) it cannot survive (c) it will never be the same (d) business will increase.

_____ 11. The majority of serious physical encounters in the workplace involve (a) co-workers (b) personal acquaintances (c) robbers (d) all of the preceding.

_____ 12. Job frustration can increase (a) productivity (b) aggression (c) promotions (d) praise.

_____ 13. Perpetrators of shooting sprees have come to be known as (a) avengers (b) workplace revenge killers (c) suffering from the postal employee syndrome (d) all of the preceding.

_____ 14. The majority of those who commit violent acts against co-workers or management have (a) made threats before (b) given no clue as to being violence prone (c) been super friendly (d) expressed suspiciously high job satisfaction.

Quiz Twenty, page 2

_____ 15. Indicators of a "toxic work environment" include (a) extreme secrecy (b) highly authoritarian management styles (c) unpredictable supervision (d) all of the preceding.

_____ 16. Workplace violence tends to begin with (a) an unexpected promotion (b) a pay raise (c) verbal harassment (d) a poor economy.

_____ 17. A recognized stress which can trigger workplace violence is (a) rapid work change (b) increased workloads (c) downsizing (d) any of the preceding.

_____ 18. What percent of violent incidents at work are preceded by threats? (a) 50% (b) 10% (c) 65% (d) 35%.

_____ 19. Some "trigger situations" that lead to violence are (a) lockouts (b) strikes (c) terminations (d) all of the preceding.

_____ 20. A stalker is described as someone who (a) makes obscene phone calls (b) has a need to intimidate (c) comes from a dysfunctional family (d) all of the preceding.

Quiz Twenty-One Name:_____

PRACTICING AND PROMOTING ETHICAL CONDUCT

Select the one best answer for each of the following and put its letter in the blank to the left.

_____ 1. Ethics has been in the spotlight in the '90s because of (a) the rapid rate of social change (b) the evolution of communications technology (c) a growing public cynicism (d) all of the preceding.

_____ 2. Standards of fair and honest conduct are known as (a) policy (b) rules and regulations (c) ethics (d) all of the preceding.

_____ 3. In a Gallup report, the occupation most people who were polled respected the most for their honesty and ethical standards was (a) senators (b) pharmacists (c) stockbrokers (d) dentists.

_____ 4. In a Gallup report, the occupation most people who were polled respected the least were (a) car sales people (b) advertising people (c) insurance sales people (d) dentists.

_____ 5. Moral standards may be (a) constructed by an individual (b) set forth by a culture (c) laid down by a religious body (d) all of the preceding.

_____ 6. What question can be asked to serve as a guideline to "ethics checks"? (a) Is it legal? (b) Is it balanced? (c) How does this make me feel about myself? (d) all of the preceding.

_____ 7. High performance companies share what one thing in common? (a) they have lots of money (b) they operate with a core set of values (c) they flaunt business ethics (d) they embarrass their competition.

_____ 8. To raise morale in a company, build a positive image and improve quality, the company must (a) do lots of advertising (b) move its products faster (c) have an ethics program (d) both a and b.

_____ 9. One accepted test for qualifying as a profession is having (a) a good Code of Ethics (b) a good plant manager (c) a high profit margin (d) a specific ratio of graduate degree holders.

_____ 10. In a Gallup poll, the virtue which topped the list of character traits that should be taught in school was (a) thrift (b) homework completion (c) self control (d) respect for others.

_____ 11. Which of these values should be considered when making a decision? (a) human flourishing (b) excuses (c) rights (d) all of the preceding.

_____ 12. For ethical standards to be understood by all employees, the standards should be (a) clear (b) unambiguous (c) written as a policy (d) all of the preceding.

_____ 13. The cost to American industry in lawsuits as a result of unethical behavior is (a) in the billions of dollars (b) in the millions of dollars (c) of minuscule value (d) not worth computing.

_____ 14. Those who report unethical or illegal behavior are known as (a) cheaters (b) whistle-blowers (c) candle sniffers (d) oilers.

_____ 15. Ethics deals with questions of (a) right and wrong (b) what is moral (c) what is immoral (d) all of the preceding.

_____ 16. Guidelines that might provide a basic ethical foundation for security leaders and their staffs might include (a) purpose or mission of the organization (b) pride in the organization (c) persistence to a commitment (d) all of the preceding.

_____ 17. The biggest factor behind the wave of ethical enlightenment is that (a) it creates chaos (b) it slows down business (c) such behavior is good for business (d) it separates the leaders from the followers.

_____ 18. The core of the decision-making/problem-solving process should be (a) values (b) a strong sense of ethics (c) both a and b (d) neither a nor b.

_____ 19. Considering the impact of litigation awards, the long-term costs of unethical shortcuts in security practices will (a) be greater than the short-term savings (b) be less than the short-term savings (c) balance the short-term savings (d) be of no concern to security managers.

_____ 20. The case of *Turner v. General Motors Corp.* was an example of the need to differentiate between (a) what is a felony and what is a misdemeanor (b) what is a crime and what is a tort (c) what is harassment and what is not harassment (d) what is illegal and what is unethical.

Quiz Twenty-Two   Name:_____

THE PRIVATE SECURITY PROFESSIONAL AND PROFESSION

Select the one best answer for each of the following and put its letter in the blank to the left.

_____ 1. The primary goal of security directors is (a) administration (b) investigation (c) management (d) all of the preceding.

_____ 2. The ultimate goal of private security is (a) apprehending those who cause losses (b) presenting a good image (c) preventing losses (d) all of the preceding.

_____ 3. An important administrative responsibility of the security director is (a) conducting background checks (b) evaluating security personnel (c) establishing security goals (d) educating employees.

_____ 4. An important investigative responsibility of the security director is (a) conducting risk analysis (b) establishing budgets (c) supervising employees (d) establishing image.

_____ 5. An important managerial responsibility of a security director is (a) conducting periodic audits (b) hiring personnel (c) establishing image (d) all of the preceding.

_____ 6. An important factor in the private security vicious circle is (a) high turn-over (b) low salaries (c) marginal personnel (d) all of the preceding.

_____ 7. A SMART objective is (a) measurable (b) relevant (c) trackable (d) all of the preceding.

_____ 8. The general guidelines of an organization are its (a) policies (b) goals (c) daily orders (d) procedures.

_____ 9. As private security becomes more specialized, use of security consultants is likely to (a) increase (b) decrease sharply (c) taper off gradually (d) remain constant.

_____ 10. General instructions detailing how employees are to conduct various aspects of their jobs are (a) policies (b) goals (c) daily orders (d) procedures.

_____ 11. To be effective, security directors must have (a) the support of top management (b) a position of authority within the organization (c) both a and b (d) neither a nor b.

_____ 12. The foundation of a security system is (a) state-of-the-art equipment (b) ample use of alarms and locks (c) well armed guards (d) the security survey.

_____ 13. According to a survey of 2,200 security officers, the most important factor in job satisfaction was (a) recognition for a job well done (b) good wages (c) flexible hours (d) a, b and c equally.

_____ 14. The Task Force on Private Security recommends that private security personnel assigned to jobs requiring firearms should requalify every (a) 6 months (b) 12 months (c) 18 months (d) 24 months.

Quiz Twenty-Two, page 2

_____ 15. Permanent signs are an effective means to (a) direct (b) educate (c) both a and b (d) neither a nor b.

_____ 16. The four "fundamental tenets of adult education" which challenge instructors to think of themselves as facilitators instead of teachers apply to (a) the hierarchy of needs (b) pedagogy (c) andragogy (d) affirmative action.

_____ 17. Actions designed to eliminate current effects of past discrimination refer to (a) the hierarchy of needs (b) pedagogy (c) andragogy (d) affirmative action.

_____ 18. Langer reports that security directors with a graduate degree (a) earn 11 percent less than those with an associate degree (b) earn about the same as those with an associate degree (c) make 37 percent more than those with an associate degree (d) are not as upwardly mobile as those with an associate degree.

_____ 19. A typical sequence in progressive discipline would go from (a) the least severe to most severe punishment (b) the most severe to least severe punishment (c) the least frequent to most frequent problem behavior (d) the most frequent to least frequent problem behavior.

_____ 20. In contrast to supervisors, managers focus on (a) short-term planning (b) the organization's mission (c) tasks to be accomplished (d) data collection.

Quiz Twenty-Three Name:_____

A LOOK TO THE FUTURE

Select the one best answer for each of the following and put its letter in the blank to the left.

_____ 1. Privatization, training and a professional image are all (a) trends in the field (b) nowhere to be found (c) something that is unattainable in private security (d) mechanisms to escape from reality.

_____ 2. Security departments contribute to additional company profits by (a) decreasing inappropriate activity (b) curtailing theft (c) decreasing the potential for lawsuits (d) all of the preceding.

_____ 3. The most striking trend in the industry today is (a) contracts (b) outsourcing (c) privatization (d) alarm systems.

_____ 4. One reason for growth in the security industry is (a) losses have been curbed (b) management is finally pro-security (c) increased fear of crime and lawsuits (d) saturation in the public police industry.

_____ 5. Police services are increasingly contracting for security services to (a) reduce operating costs (b) reduce overhead (c) increase service to the general public (d) all of the preceding.

_____ 6. The percentage of private security officers who are armed today is about (a) 10% (b) 20% (c) 40% (d) 75%.

_____ 7. More value is being put on preemployment screening because of (a) the response to workplace violence (b) negligent hiring (c) substance abuse (d) all of the preceding.

_____ 8. The security officer of the future will (a) be better paid (b) receive more training (c) have higher standards (d) all of the preceding.

_____ 9. Future private security officers will be classroom trained in (a) fire-life safety codes (b) basic criminal laws (c) investigative techniques (d) all of the preceding.

_____ 10. The future progressive private security officer will carry (a) a personal digital communicator (b) a firearm (c) a nightstick (d) pepper grenades.

_____ 11. The most obvious trend in the future of private security is (a) computerized mapping (b) belt-pack video recorders (c) expansion of global markets (d) new type card access devices.

_____ 12. The word "rightsizing" means (a) segregating departments from one another (b) absorbing other staff functions such as health, safety and facilities management (c) considering international implications (d) all of the preceding.

_____ 13. Technology (a) has raised skill levels (b) has suppressed change (c) has been slow to be accepted (d) is an intuitive tool.

Quiz Twenty-Three, page 2

_____ 14. Ethics programs in business have proven to be effective in reducing incidents of (a) fraud (b) the abuse of intellectual property (c) other corporate crime (d) all of the preceding.

_____ 15. Security managers in the future must (a) be more cautious about new technology (b) forget about cultural diversity (c) be better risk-takers (d) none of the preceding.

_____ 16. Currently private security is provided in the form of (a) contract (b) proprietary (c) hybrid (d) all of the preceding.

_____ 17. Hybrid security is a form of security that (a) combines contract and proprietary security (b) uses rent-a-cop types with no preemployment screening (c) uses technology and personnel (d) is used only in emergency situations.

_____ 18. Today's security officer can be best described as (a) a young person (b) a high school graduate who may have some college (c) one who has met minimum training standards (d) all of the preceding.

_____ 19. Today private security employs (a) more than three times as many people as law enforcement (b) more than five times as many people as law enforcement (c) nearly one-half as many people as law enforcement (d) the same number of people as law enforcement.

_____ 20. The Wackenhut Private Security Corporation has recently opened its (a) 1st detention facility (b) 22nd detention facility (c) 45th detention facility (d) 99th detention facility.